# WHEELS OF STEEL

## A ROLLERCOASTER RIDE OF ADVENTURES BY ROAD AND BY RAIL

# JIM TAYLOR

*Wheels of Steel*

Published by The Conrad Press in the United Kingdom 2019

Tel: +44(0)1227 472 874
www.theconradpress.com
info@theconradpress.com

ISBN 978-1-911546-60-3

Cover illustrations by Maria Priestley.

Typesetting and design by: Charlotte Mouncey, www.bookstyle.co.uk

The Conrad Press logo was designed by Maria Priestley.

Printed and bound in Great Britain
by Clays Ltd, Elcograf S.p.A.

# INTRODUCTION

I t's great to be a passenger, but if you're the driver then you control your own destiny. I learned to drive the little farm tractor we had when I was a child and that was my introduction. Living in the countryside, it was essential to be in charge of your own transport and motorbikes were much less fun in the winter months.

I was born in a gamekeeper's cottage on the Berkshire Downs in midwinter. We didn't have a car until I was four years old, when my family moved to rural Kent. I spent a hard childhood growing up on a rundown smallholding, on which we struggled to make a subsistence living doing things the right way. I loved the old-fashioned pioneering spirit it evoked, we were as self-sufficient as it was possible to be, but it couldn't be sustained on the small amount of land we farmed. We never had a family holiday and I knew I would have to get out there and grab a future as soon as I was able. I had a handful of first best friends from my wasted school days and together we made the roads our domain. All of a sudden life was great for a few years and then it was all gone, as people got married and grew up, had their own families and I was left wondering where it all went.

I found my calling in the early 90s as the 'New World Order' was running into trouble; it was the break-up of Yugoslavia and war on Europe's doorstep. Full of compassionate zeal and a belief in the 'Global Village', I outfitted a small truck and drove it to the front line, packed full of humanitarian aid and good intentions. It is that part of the story that I really wanted to tell: when there was hope for the future and a better world. I was by no means alone and the vivid, memorable and often ridiculous characters driving the same roads were what made the 90s for me.

Post Cold War, pre millennial mayhem! And it was so great, a far cry from plucking turkeys and digging potatoes.

Jim Taylor, Kent, November 2018

# CONTENTS

# PROLOGUE

My diary (which I had kept up almost every day from my early teens to the late 1990s) reads:

**5ᵗʰ September 1983**
'Sunday, watched *Mad Max* again twice and *The Warriors*. I worked in the tea rooms, and an hour picking stones in the field. They gave me £8.00.'

I had just started the sixth-form at Brockhill and St Leonards Secondary Modern and was dropping out as fast as I could. The mates I was hanging around with were predominantly those, like me, who had just got their first bikes on the road and we were showing off (as best as we knew how) at every opportunity. We were a motley collection of suspects, and most of us wore our new leather jackets everywhere; just like 'the bronze' in that cult classic road movie mentioned in my diary entry.

There was Aggi on his FS1-E, Chris Woods on an RD 50 that he had fitted with an oversize front sprocket – he claimed this brought his top speed up above 50mph. But only after a mile-long downhill section of Stone Street from the bottom of Hempton Hill to the Drum PH, flat on the tank with no wind shear. Dave 'The Gooba' had gone straight to a 100cc TS and wouldn't let anyone near it. Jase (Woody) and Jethrow had the jackets, but never did get the bikes after all their talk. They each bought MK1 Escorts as soon as they turned seventeen.

Later on that same week in September, Chris and I paid £15 for an old Austen 1300 with no brakes, from the local scrap yard. We ripped it around the field like idiots each evening after school, neither of us really knew how to drive. My diary entries for the following week read:

### Sunday 2nd October
'We lost all our forward gears & stuck the car in reverse & we spun it around like that. Chris accidentally ran the door & front wheel right diagonally across my body. But I am alright.'

### Monday 3rd October
'After school John Read came up & we ripped the car around, shot it up, sledge hammered it & I spun it into the Transit.'

### Tuesday 4th October
'I got myself merry on snake-bite, then had a good chat with Kerry in private study. I wrote off the car today by ripping the grill off and busting the suspension off one side of the steering.'

### Wednesday 5th October
'We ripped the doors off Sampson's, Martyn's and Lawrence's lockers cause they had locks & we don't. I bought Fergus's Dance Craze LP off him for £2.75.'

### Thursday 6th October
'I brought my boxing gloves to PE, sparred with Fergus, Tim Cudby & Ian Squire. Then no one would fight me.'

Actually, the week after that, Fergus hit me twice in the mouth, forcing my teeth deep into the top of my tongue. Then I knew why boxers wore gum shields and I got myself one. I was really into the idea of being a boxer and used to spar with Justin Rigby during our PE lessons. It's funny because both of us had spent the previous three years pretty much refusing to involve ourselves in games whatsoever. Decades later I learned that Rigby had joined the army after leaving school and had gone on to become a regimental champion. He thanked me for those early bouts and seemed to have forgiven me for sticking a thumb in his eye.

**Early motoring recollections, circa 1970**

My early recollections of motoring are mostly of us breaking down and of me being car-sick. I was not a good traveller and just the smell of that vinyl interior was enough to bring on the nausea, even before the engine started.

When I was very young Dad had this little old mini. I remember a drive across open land on a very long gravel drive or track way, I don't know where, but it was nowhere near home I'm sure. To me it went on for miles, but was probably only a few hundred yards. This grit was flicking up from the little tyres and pinging against the undercarriage – I was terrified, as I was sure that the car was breaking up.

In the same mini, Dad drove us all out onto a deep shingle beach (probably out by Dungeness) and of course, we got our wheels dug in and were well and truly stuck. My older sister Lyn and I were worried that we would never get off and the sea would come in and swallow our car up. We needed quite a bit of help from a group of beach trippers we flagged down to push and dig us out that day.

# PART ONE
# EARLY MAYHEM

# CHAPTER 1: GO ON DAD, DO A HUNDRED

Cars had never suited me as naturally as bikes had, I was twenty one before I got my first barely legal wreck on the road. I'd grown up with an array of old bangers that Dad had bought cheap; my view was that four wheels were useful, but unreliable and maintenance intensive.

The earliest of my motoring recollections is probably Dad racing through the lanes in his dark blue Mk 2 Jaguar with its big bull nose and chromed figurehead of a deadly animal leaping for the kill. There was me, as a four year old, egging him on, 'Go on Dad, do a hundred', and he would. He was a good driver, better than I would ever be, and looked the part; neat beard, shades, and a well groomed DA hairstyle to keep those dark curls at bay. He had an eagle tattoo on his right bicep, silhouetted by a red setting sun, a pouncing tiger on the left forearm. My dad was a smart talker and a hard worker, and I've never seen anyone jive like him and Mum.

We had the right car for the right time; Dad had made a load of money, very quickly, when he and Mickey Vav (a little Greek rocker he had been at school with) created 'Taylor-Vavlitis Ltd.', which was a company that ran for a year or more, out of our back shed. A group of Mum and Dad's friends mixed and packaged pharmaceuticals that Dad sold to poultry farms on a huge mark up.

With that money from the business and what they could borrow from relatives, plus a collection of green shield stamps, my parents were able to put down the deposit for our own smallholding. Six acres of derelict chicken farm covered with stinging nettles, ticks and red mite. The place took some cleaning up. I have some vivid recollections of one Saturday, when we ripped the rotted wooden floor out from one of our sheds in the yard; ten rats came up with every plank. We had Dad and Uncle Chris with shotguns, our faithful Labrador-Retriever, Bob and a couple of Jack Russells on the starting line. George the butcher had been a lodger with us, he was young, tall and gangly and wore cobble glasses. I remember him losing his glasses and jumping around with the pitch-fork, scared of the rats and trying not to get shot, while myself and big sis Lyn went after the stragglers with clubs, finishing them off where we could find 'em. That afternoon we killed well over a hundred rats between us. If there is one of God's creatures I hate more than anything else, it's rats, and I've learned to deal with them over the years without any of the compassionate restrictions I reserve for other wild creatures whatsoever.

We didn't have a tractor then and the Jag wasn't much use on the land, so Dad got hold of a little Series 1 Land Rover pickup. The cab itself was just a tarpaulin and I liked that little truck better than any other car we ever had. I never felt sick in it, there was plenty of fresh air and no horrible plastic smell. Dad drove it through the sea of stingers in the field, with me standing up in the back, to carve out trails. We used it as a battering ram to demolish one of the old sheds in the well field. That was great fun, but we broke all the rear lights into the bargain. Dad was a genius, but he was also a maniac, and absolutely incorrigible.

The other car from my childhood, of which I have fond memories, is my Grandad's little 1969 mini van. He had converted it into a station wagon, with side windows and a folding rear seat kit. My mum's parents, we called them

Nanny and Grandad, used to drive this little toy car from Eastbourne to Stowting (about fifty miles) to visit us once a month. It took them more than three hours and I don't think Grandad ever took it over 38 mph. They always made a stop off for a picnic lunch of brown bread sandwiches in little squares, a thermos flask of tea and some apples, spread out on a tweed blanket beside the canal near Appledore. I still have Grandad's mini, stuck away in the barn, awaiting completion of a restoration I began in 2003.

Dad had a white mini pickup for a short time in the early 80s; he had bought it from Mickey Andrews. Mick was a family friend who emigrated to Canada to live with his Native American wife, Joyce. She was a pure blood 'Red Indian' squaw, with a genuine scar on her thigh from an arrow wound! He had brought her to England to get married and they camped in our wood for the whole summer holidays: it was great. That car didn't last long and it went up in flames when Chris Carey brought some gas welding gear round.

We always seemed to have one car drivable, one being worked on and at least two dead ones still lying about, waiting for the scrap man. The Vauxhall Viva was quite a good car, until my sister Lyn and I washed it one Christmas Eve, we'd hosed through the grill at the top of the bonnet, not thinking about the electrics under there. It didn't want to start that night when Dad had to take us all to Dover. He had to do his shift on the P&O ferry named the 'Tiger' that was sitting in port. We got there eventually, but the 'Merry Christmas' we'd written on the bonnet in lipstick stained into the white paint and was a hell of a job to scrub off.

The Viva was superseded by a white Triumph Toledo; that lasted only a matter of months before it needed new wheel bearings. An expert back-street mechanic by the name of Martin Pointer came over to do the job. Martin jacked it up onto blocks and removed the old bearings, then he disappeared and we didn't see him again for months. He was a good mechanic and a family friend too, we always used him, but he did have this habit of disappearing every now and then, going off to buy parts, or cigarettes or something, then never coming back to finish the job. Whenever he did reappear he was always so cheerful and it was hard not to forgive him for his unreliability.

We had a goat once that used to pull washing off the line, as well as other annoying stuff. Martin was over and had spent all day on our Renault 12 TL, having filled all the dents and primed it ready for re-spraying. The goat ran right over the car from bonnet to boot, leaving cloven hoof marks over the prepared surface like some kind of racing stripe. On another occasion, that same goat took the opportunity of munching through the wiring on one of our other cars, while the bonnet was up and we were all having a tea break.

That Renault 12 was one of our best cars and lasted maybe two years, altogether we had three of them to tide us over during the mid 80s. There was also a Datsun 180B Coupé that we got from some scrap men, but the vehicle we had the best use out of was an old Mk 1 Ford Transit: a 1600 petrol, flat-back truck with teakwood rear and side gates that we hand painted in 'true blue'. That's the one I actually learned to drive around the field on my own in. I used it when I was fifteen or sixteen to load up with logs that I'd dragged out of the wood, just to get them down to the house. I did mess up once with the clutch and the accelerator pedals: whilst turning left into a gateway, I slammed it into the post, which cracked it and threw my head against the windscreen, but didn't break the truck.

Two other vehicles of character I remember from that

time included the Citroen 2CV, which ended up buried in our front garden upside down. The plan had been for it to act as a hollow structure for the garden soak-away we needed. The system was never connected and it wouldn't have worked in clay anyway.

The police did come round once, regarding that car, in connection with a murder enquiry in Essex, I believe. It can't have been a strong connection as they didn't want to dig it up. The car is still there, under a few tons of extra clay and topsoil that has now sunk into an interesting bowl shaped feature.

By far the most interesting of Dad's old cars was a Peugeot 404 pickup, in off-white. The gears were on the steering column like old American cars. Mum crashed it soon after passing her driving test, crunching the off-side headlamp surround. Martin Pointer patched it up and Mickey Vav fabricated a rear shelter that looked like a dog kennel, made out of box section and sheet steel, all painted in red oxide. It sat on the pickup base like a little red house and made the whole thing look very hillbilly. We all loved that truck, including Patch the dog, who would sit up in the passenger seat when mum took it to the stores. It was sad to see the old thing go in the end; I don't think Dad ever actually sold a car that still ran, they all went for scrap.

# CHAPTER 2: THE SELLINDGE SWAN ANGELS

The summer of 1985 started with me bikeless for a short while. I was eighteen; I was also jobless, having chucked in my job at Dudley Holt's farm in Stanford. I had worked like a slave for a month, as Wilf Missing's labourer, twelve hours a day, seven days a week. We worked under the foremanship of Wilf's father (also named Wilf). He had a big bushy beard and hair to match, his front teeth were missing, knocked out by a pig they said. I didn't talk with him too much, I was one of Little Willie's (young Wilf's younger brother) friends, and he didn't seem to approve. The only thing that made Wilf senior grin was the recollection of tales of hardship from his working life – that and watching me or some other poor soul struggling around the yard with impossible weights and loads. We got through four other labourers during that month of May, none of them lasted a week, so I think I must have done alright.

Dudley was a slave driver and I got all the worst jobs; smashing up the old concrete driveway with a sledge hammer, then running up and down the yard with full wheel barrows of wet concrete to construct Dudley's nuclear fall-out shelter. I knocked myself flat once, pushing the barrow under some low scaffolding. It carried on and I was left on my back with a headache. When he wouldn't give me a raise after that first month, I jacked the job in. I went straight down to Folkestone and signed on, and then I went and got myself a grade one skinhead. I started hanging around in the precinct and down the front with the other yobs, I was eighteen, but before I could get sucked back into that dead end lifestyle, an event occurred that changed everything.

Since the end of the previous year, one of my earliest friends from Stowting Primary School, Phillip Andrews, had begun turning up at Sellindge Sports and Social Club. My local crowd used to go to all the regular parties they held up there and they were always good fun. Phil had turned teetotal and only drank peppermint and lemonade; he was always so cheerful he didn't need alcohol to have a laugh, and we always had plenty to laugh about.

Most of the 'boy racers' wanted Ford Escorts to show off in, but Phil was different. His first car had been a 1950s Morris Minor, one of the very early ones with the mechanically protractible signal arms instead of indicator lights. Phil had turned up at the club with a bright orange Skoda 110R Coupé, it was the same colour as his hair. We did sort of like it as it looked a bit like a Porsche at the back. With its rear-mounted engine and sporty alloy wheels, when most other cars still had hubcaps, it was kind of cool. It didn't look so good from the front though, as if the designers had chopped it off a foot too short, then stuck the wrong lights into the blanked-off end.

The car was only an 1100 but we still got it over 100 mph, just, with four-up on the newly built M20 section between Ashford and Folkestone. Skoda have got a pretty good name now, but back then when the cold war was still on, the rep was along the lines of a confidence comparison between the MZ marque and say, Suzuki – well that's how a motorcyclist could explain the street cred gap. It was usually me, Phil, Jethrow and Little Willie: out most nights, and the sound track was from *The Wanderers*, we knew it all by heart.

Phil was a cowman at Moorstock Farm and loved to get out and about, his drug was the road, on two wheels or four.

It was the weekend of the Kent Custom Bike Show, held up on Stowting common, and my second year up there. Dave (the Gooba) had suggested we went down to Brabourne, the neighbouring village, to raise hell at a village hall disco that Saturday night – so it was on.

Four of us piled into the Skoda and drove down there in high spirits: Phil, Dave, Will and myself. There was a new boy in town (actually he had been in the village for probably two years), Will's mate from school, who Dave had recently befriended. 'Del from Hell' we christened him, he was from an army family that had come back home from some town in Germany. Del had just got a new bike and wanted to show it off, a Honda CM 125 factory custom that looked good to us at the time. He was so proud of that bike, we let him tag along; it was just as well that he had to leave early that night, although he missed the fun, the bike made it home safe.

The party was going well and we'd even been chatting to some of the Brabourne casuals, but they didn't like us taking an interest in the local girls. It went bad after Will knocked a drink over someone's girlfriend and laughed. The rest of us were just being ourselves. One of their lot told me we needed to leave, or Will was 'going to get his head kicked in'. I told him that wasn't going to happen and that we weren't going anywhere. His response was 'There's only four of you and there's thirty of us, so you'd better fuck off now'. 'Bollocks' I said, 'we're staying', and I went to warn the others. They already knew, and we stood in the middle of the dance floor with half of Brabourne village staring us down.

The track playing right then was that tribal beat thing

by *Santana* 'Jingo, jingo lo ba-ba, lo ba-ba, lo ba-ba, lo ba'. It thumped out as we danced. We turned it into a sort of a war dance, side by side the four of us, stamping our Steel Magnum boots to the beat and staring straight back at them. When the music stopped, I said to get our jackets while we could and put them in the car, then we'd come back in and face up to whatever was going to happen.

We got out into the car park and stowed our gear, when dozens of them came herding out, shouting and jeering; they thought we had chickened out. I shouted that we were coming back inside and if they wanted it we would take them on 'one on one, come on then'. I was between the Skoda and another parked car and the first idiot who ran the corridor took my best right hander. I actually saw him knocked sideways, like a swing door. But the gap filled and I was fighting two at a time in front of me, I don't know if it was always the same two, as there were plenty of refills behind them, trying to push through. It was pretty confusing, but I didn't give any ground. Then I felt blows from behind me and I knew Dave wasn't there anymore. The space was too confined and I couldn't fight off attackers from both ends on my own. I felt the press of bodies and blows coming down on me from overhead, I was still fighting, but starting to get pushed down lower and it wasn't good.

Then I was being pulled up by some huge bloke and the crowd was moving back. Some of the older blokes from the village seemed to be breaking it all up, and just in time I reckoned.

It turned out that Phil knew a bloke called Toomey, who had gone out with the sister of a mate of ours we called 'Woody'. Well that connection had saved our bacon. I looked around and Dave was limping back towards the car. I saw someone whack him in the back of the head, then run back to the crowd, lambs! Someone else got a last punch in on me (that was from behind too) whilst Toomey still had a hold of me. I checked on Phil, who still had his car keys in his hand and we decided we were ready to leave. I don't know what happened to Will, but I was relieved to see him when I got in the car too. The mob started chucking handfuls of gravel, and a couple of kicks went in as Phil took the wheel, but we made it out okay.

There was a bloody nose or two between us and I had a good black eye. My Fred Perry shirt was torn, but overall, I think we came out of it pretty well. The car had a couple of dents and a windscreen wiper arm was broken. I was later told by Sean Lincoln (he had friends in Brabourne) that the first one I'd hit had ended up on our bonnet and got the wiper arm snagged up in his Pringle jumper.

To cap it all, we all received visits from the Brabourne village cop, PC Carr, who tried to get us bound over to keep the peace. He claimed we had hit another car whilst making our exit. Well who could prove it, or blame us if we did in any case. I don't know, nothing came of it.

That fight forged a bond between the four of us, and along with Del (who swore he'd be there next time) we had our gang. We all fashioned cut-offs with 'Sellindge' marked on the back and decided to call ourselves the 'Magnums'. There were other periphery members, who were keen (in varying degrees) to support us in any new forays we might plan: Heapsey, Tritton, the Keeble brothers, Woody, Shane Tibbles and Lee Belfield. But they couldn't wear the cuts; it was our gang of five.

A year later, after Phil died in a motorcycle crash, we dropped the name and I painted mine over with flames where the name was, leaving 'Sellindge' at the top. I still have my denim original, I wore it till the end of that decade and also on a handful of old time occasions.

That winter which followed the glorious summer of 85 was long and cold. We established ourselves as *the* resident hell-raisers of the Sellindge Sports and Social Club and we were more than ready to start procedures for a summer war with Brabourne. We managed to get banned from one of their pubs (the Plough) for turning up mob-handed in two cars one wet night, looking for anyone on the list we'd drawn up. They weren't in there that night, but a pint glass did get broken. I knocked it off the table by accident just as we were leaving and I tried to cushion its fall by sticking my foot out. It would have worked if I had been wearing slippers, but not with Steel Magnums.

In April, things had started heating up after Will bought a Hillman Avenger from a reprobate called Chip. Chip, Martin and Colin were greasy rat-pack bikers from Smeeth just down the road and we'd recently made acquaintance with them. Chip was the same type as Will, from a hillbilly family, working on farms and buying a string of scrap yard cars that were on their last legs just to get them to the end of the month. Del was on a YTS (Youth Training Scheme) attachment to Sellindge Service Station and he would routinely fill their cars up for them, then give them all their money back as change.

We had some fun in that Avenger, it became the club car, as Phil had sold his Skoda and was getting heavily into his bikes. We were all progressing naturally from 125s to 250s, to 400cc proper motorcycles, whatever we could afford. The club car though was always a community example of our gang's pride.

The day Will bought that car, we did the rounds of the local villages. Lyminge had a chip shop, the others only pubs, but they were alive back then. Any night of the week you could have a good time and no one worried then about driving with a skin full, if you stayed out of the towns you were going to be alright. I don't think most people even considered it wrong; the barman might look after your keys if you couldn't walk, talk or stay on a barstool, but only if he liked you.

We ended up driving slowly past the 'Blue Anchor' ('Blue Wanker', as we called that particular Brabourne pub). We believed their lot would be drinking in there on that Thursday night. An empty milk bottle got thrown from the car, smashing the window to their pool room. Within seconds, blokes were bundling out of the front door and Will put his foot down. I saw about ten of them come out as we sped off. It was as if we had broken open a hornets' nest. We noticed very quickly that there were sets of headlights bearing down fast behind us. Will drove flat-out along the country lanes for a couple of miles before we started to lose them. We went back to Del's house for beers and thought we'd got away with it. So stupid, things like that can escalate and as nineteen year olds, fired up on beer and speed, you don't see sense at all, just what feels right at the time – which is usually wrong.

My diary entry for the next day, Friday 18th April reads:

'We went from the club to the Tiger & Dave nicked a picture out of the bogs. Then on the way to the Chinky we had a flat, so we had to lift the car & change the wheel. Denis was pissed up on 3 pints & we were all messing around in the Chinky & I pushed Denis out the door & he fell over his own feet. We then went back to Phil's. We slept there'

Will only had a wheel brace, no jack, so we all had to

grab hold of parts of the bodywork and lift the front wing up, high enough for Will to do the change.

Denis was just one of Del's nicknames: Desmond Dekker and Dingo were others; his real name was Derek Harbottle.

The following day, six of us got together to plan our attendance at the next Brabourne village hall do. We had a council of war in my shed, where I suggested upping it considerably, as we would doubtlessly be seriously outnumbered.

I wanted the others to wait in the car park, while I walked into the hall to lure them out. Tool handles and bottles seemed to make sense, but I wanted something more 'A Team'. I formed this brilliant plan: to douse a section of the road leading out of the village with petrol, and have the Avenger parked a short distance beyond. I said we could get them to chase a couple of us up the road and when we had cleared the danger zone, the team by the car would throw petrol bombs over our heads, turning the road between us and them into an inferno. The intention was to create a huge incident, without actually trying to kill anyone – although we had considered shotguns in the car in case things went wrong.

The next day, a couple of the more sensible members managed to persuade the rest that the battle plan carried a massive potential for fuck-ups, and we would all likely go to prison whatever happened.

Two days later, I was outside Shane's row of houses in Greenfields and a car pulled up. George was a flash black man I'd known from primary school; in fact he was virtually the only black man most of us had known. Coming from a small village in East Kent in the 1980s, it wasn't surprising he was a bit of a local celebrity. George drove a black Opal Manta and wore gold chains; he pretty much ticked all the clichés. But he had been a biker a few years prior; along with Wilf Missing and a bunch of others who weren't that much older than us, they had started a club called the 'Sellindge Warriors'. They'd been a five man band too, with a reputation for getting into scrapes and throwing parties we all remembered.

George warned me that two car loads of blokes from Brabourne had been down the Dukes Head and the Swan (the two Sellindge pubs on the main road) looking for us on Monday night. George had known that we were all up at the club but hadn't let on. He did say that the Sellindge shop had had a window broken that same night. That made me feel bad; it was a small village and everyone knew each other's business.

A couple of nights later a few of us were having a drink up at Del's house, we were up in his bedroom, window open, heavy metal on the deck. Two cars drove up the road slow enough for us to take notice, then discount it. The next thing we knew they were back: it was them alright, a Mk 3 Capri and a Ford Escort van crawling past our Avenger that was parked on Swan Lane. Missiles were thrown as we scrabbled for weapons, and someone jumped out the back of the van and put a brick through our windscreen. They were long gone before we could get outside.

Del's dad was none too pleased (he would have been less impressed if he had known the full story) and we knew we had brought this down. I went straight to my own family's home and sat low at the top of our drive for an hour or so with a loaded shotgun – they would get more than they bargained for if they showed up at our place. My dad wanted to know what I was up to out there, gone midnight. He was not best pleased either when I confessed the whole thing. Dad always knew what to do for the best and he was never afraid to do what was right.

This situation could easily have progressed to cars being torched, houses targeted and maybe people getting killed. All because some tosser splashed a drink over a girl a year past, at a party we weren't even invited to. Even so, Will and I still wanted to find their cars and do them. Phil actually came round for me on a wet night, camouflaged up, with a balaclava and some bolt croppers. He wanted to find the Capri and Escort in their pub car park and cut the brake pipes. I had to admire his commitment and it was his car that got damaged in the first place but... Well we didn't do it.

My dad went to the Blue Anchor (he wouldn't let me come) and laid down the law to their crowd, with the approval of the pub landlady. The iron was pulled out of the fire.

There was only one other incident, a few weeks later. Dave had his 21st birthday party at Sellindge village hall and the black Capri turned up outside. It sat there on the main road and words were exchanged, but then it drove off sharpish when Woody and I strode out towards them. We all car'd up and trawled the lanes for a while but they were gone, honour satisfied all round.

We were out every night of the week looking for action; there were always parties to crash and band nights at the local pubs, several nights a week. It was a great time to be young and mobile and it didn't matter if you had a windscreen or not. We got a replacement from a scrap car two days after the incident, it cost us a beer each and we'd only had to drive it one night without. That was the night of the Stowting Peace Rooms barn dance.

We were all wearing full face crash hats for the drive over

there in the rain, and we walked in with boots and back patches, to discover that it was a respectable church do. The 'barn dancers' were ranging in age from about forty to seventy-plus and included my old primary school headmaster Mr Deacon with his wife and their grandchildren.

We had to get drunk quick, it was so embarrassing it was funny. But eventually we had a great time, no one was without a dance partner and Dave won a basket of fruit in the raffle. We did throw some of it at him, but on the whole we toned it down a fair bit. The folk were happy enough with us there and we got invited to church for the next morning – and we went. We had to stop on the way there for me to be sick though.

The summer went on and as I said, we lost Phil. This devastated us and the whole village was affected, nothing was the same again. Although he came across as madcap, Phil was actually the most responsible out of the lot of us: absolutely incorruptible, with a clear sense of right and wrong. For a long time afterwards, every Sunday, we would visit his parents Andy and Pauline and chat all evening with them and Tania (his younger sister). He was too good to be forgotten.

Shane left to join the army and Tony Heaps took his place in the group line-up. We were on the bikes more often than not, as it was harvest season and Will was working all hours. He didn't get freed off again 'til October and no-one else owned a car. Will called me in to work on the potato harvester at Walkers' farm, where he took on the charge hand role. The crew consisted of, among others, Robert Hands (Handyman), Greeny, and as fate would have it, my old girlfriend Sarah. Will drove the harvester and we stood on it sorting the spuds from the stones and lumps of mud as they came through.

I had taken eight months getting over Sarah and I was fine. Well that first Thursday was payday and the team all went out; that was enough to do it and I was right back in the frying pan. It lasted longer than I thought it would, but ultimately she wanted children and I was scared stiff of getting hurt again.

Will had got himself a new heap of shit; a Toyota with tyres so worn that the wire mesh was showing through on the edges. We were back to being out every night; Will and whichever girl would ride with him, me and Sarah, Greeny, Tony and Rob. That usually meant that someone had to ride in the boot or on the bonnet between pubs. This was madness, but such fun – it went on every night of the potato harvest and we always spent every penny we had earned.

Dave and Del were always on their bikes and we would meet up with the likes of Wobble, little Craig Tibbles, Tritton and the Keeble lads at any of the Sellindge pubs.

I remember one night we were coming back from a party at Lympne, with a car load, and we had Tony and Greeny in the boot. Will was driving like a maniac to shake them up. Then he took it off road. The old teenage meeting place, near Keebles' house was referred to as 'down the brook'. Kids used to get over there on bicycles, as there were banks, mud, tree roots and jumps to play around on. The poor bastards in the boot were shouting for help as we bounced around the tracks, and when we stopped and opened up, Tone was all dazed but Greeny was laughing like a mad puppet. So we put him on the roof like a flying squirrel, and did the course again. He would *not* fall off! This experiment started off a craze for roof surfing between pubs. Rob and I would climb out of opposite windows simultaneously, reach out across the roof to lock hands and pull ourselves up and out, while Will drove at 70mph along Swan Lane. He even did a handbrake turn at this speed with Greeny clinging onto the roof; nothing could shake that boy off.

This couldn't go on, and it didn't. Within a couple of weeks, Will had rolled his car down Hythe hill on the way to the Chinky. Somehow he and Tone had both ended up out of the car, and then Tony nearly got himself run down, blundering around in the road. Del was alright, he'd been in the back with his new girlfriend Lynne. He must have had his seat belt on. She went to hospital with the others, a genuine case of whiplash. Will was kept in for several days with a head injury and the Toyota was written off.

Will went on to crash a string of cars he'd bought with some compensation money he'd come into; Walkers' farm had paid him off after his hand got mangled in the potato riddler. Then a couple of years later the fool got himself married, without telling anyone, and disappeared for twenty years. He turned up like a bad penny eventually: divorced and skint, but he still had that gleam in his eye.

# CHAPTER 3: ROAD WARRIORS

F ast foreword another year and the line-up had changed:
A friend of mine called Chip was taking a bunch of
us out to the Bull in Bethersden; he was driving the car he
had just bought that day. Music: one of Tony's tapes went
into the cassette player and it ate it, the dashboard started
smoking and there was a scramble to pick the thing out and
chuck it out the window.

The Bull was a nice country pub, you'd think, by the look
of it: picnic tables and window boxes. It probably was on
a Sunday afternoon, but on a Friday night that summer it
was the newest and greatest biker hang out. Anyone into
the nomad scene would get down there at some point; it
was mobility and the ability to not give a fuck. The town
was for pretty boys and tarts in Ra-Ra skirts, but we ruled
the lanes and the out of the way places, in worn out jeans
and army shirts.

On the way back, we took a short cut through a farm
yard and Chip ploughed through the edge of a muck heap
for a laugh, sending fresh manure into the air, as well as
ramming it through the front grill, the fan throwing it all
over the engine so we got the hit of it coming through the
air vents. We ended up in an open field racing around after
rabbits in the headlights, doors ajar and everyone ready to
jump out and catch their own. Of course we never got close
to anything, but we did manage to get ourselves stuck. With
everyone out there pushing and Chip screaming the engine,

burning deep ruts in the soft turf to get us back up the slope, we were going to make it. Then the engine cut out.

Lifting the bonnet in the dark, we could see one contributing factor; the exhaust manifold was glowing bright orange. The engine wouldn't turn on the key, so there was nothing for it but to push the thing back down the hill and hope we could bump it into life before the farmer or the cops arrived. The motor popped and burbled and then took on some life and three leather clad rejects ran along behind, not daring to stop 'til we got it around and up to the gate. We were half ruined by the time we slouched back into the vehicle, sweating like apes, and Chip was the only one still laughing. He turned round and said 'I think it's about time I was getting a new car'.

My first car, after finally passing my test on the second attempt, was a brilliant first car. I'd had a gardening job, one day a week, going for six or seven months, at a posh Tudor house in Warehorne, just south of Ashford. I always rode my old Honda CB200 the fifteen miles or so, along the back roads at full throttle all the way. This ex-police bike had started off looking very respectable, but two years of extreme abuse had reduced it to something resembling a crushed beer crate on two wheels. I'd given up taxing and insuring it and I hadn't MOT'd it once.

The upper class family at Parsonage Farm were not the sort I was used to working or mixing with, but we got on alright. They kept on at me about sorting my transport out and I took no notice. When their daughter's car failed its MOT, I was offered it, in exchange for two days work. The Datsun 100A estate was not without style, although this one was an unattractive yellow colour. It had a few months' tax left on it, which was key. We manhandled my bike into the back of it, lying on its side and I drove off feeling quite pleased with myself.

I'd only got five miles down the road before the exhaust back box came off. I pulled up, ran back for it and picked it up, burning my hands in the process.

It was November '87 and I was living at 'Kestrels', a communal house off the main Ashford to Hythe road, it was one of the only rent-a-room properties in Sellindge village. The owner of the place was an Irishman named Rodger, he was very easygoing and hardly ever there. Rodger had allowed me to build a small shed under the hedge in the front garden to keep my bikes in, being a bike enthusiast too. He turned a blind eye to our obvious party antics; as long as we cleaned up afterwards, so that it was fit for him to spend his Sundays there with his girlfriend, it was okay.

We always replaced broken items, like doors and light shades, as and when they got smashed. I remember Rodger turning up one day as Wozzy was just fitting a replacement internal door – he got them from work and we needed one every couple of months. Wozzy was a builder, and Stu (the other house-mate) worked at the butchers down the road.

Sellindge was an odd place, there was no actual centre to it and my generation were a right mixed bunch. Kestrels was only 500 yards from the Dukes Head, which was handy as we had all been banned from the Club, 'for life' earlier in the year. When the other village pub, the Swan, had changed hands the previous year and been renamed the Mucky Duck, several of us had been banned from there too. Once the new landlord had established himself and earned the respect of the locals, we were all allowed back in. I got myself banned again six months later, after a tussle with little Craig and a smashed beer glass. It probably wouldn't have mattered had it been late in the evening with the till full already. Very soon 'the Duck' had earned a reputation as the greatest live band venue in the area and a bit of a biker hang out. They knew that if you dropped a pint you were going to buy another straight away.

That November I went to the first big party thrown by the newly formed *Oakmen* motorcycle club of Ashford. The venue was at a place called the Lodge, in Charing. I went there with Chip, Martin Greenhill, Tony and Greasy Colin. Everyone who rode bikes was there and it was the start of something big. Although I never formally joined, I went to their parties as a hang-around, and there was a group of them who would turn up whenever I had a do on back at the farm. They were a good club and the 80s were good days.

Having a flat space shelter on wheels proved useful, as I discovered I could pick things up along the way, things that seemed to have been left abandoned by the side of the road. My moral reasoning was a little blinkered during that period of my life, for various apparently justifiable reasons. I didn't have a problem with the poll tax when it came along, it seemed fair, but road tax, I deeply resented that, as I owned several bikes too, and was expected to pay for each when I was only going to use one at a time. I considered it fair pickings when I found myself a wheelbarrow, the odd bucket, a bit of rope, and definitely anything left out by council workers. Road working equipment and materials was particularly enticing, I reckoned that I could get better use out of stuff than the authorities who were installing it. I was particularly looking out for concrete slabs to floor out my new motorbike shed. Once that was sorted, I started laying a path of slabs across the lawn to it, then a parking platform beside the shed.

One evening I took Chip and Martin up the Sports and Social Club driveway just before kicking out time. I got them to help me run off with three slabs from the new patio that had been laid right beside the door. They thought we were just going to pick them up from a pile, not lift them from the ground: they couldn't believe what we were doing and that we were getting away with it. That was what was so funny about it.

Of course I regret all that now and can hardly believe we did some of the stupid things we did. I told myself it was all part of preparing for the breakdown of society. Armageddon, the War of the Worlds. We had no idea that the cold war would come crashing down with the Berlin Wall within two years, opening up a whole new world of hope and aspirations, also that the end of the world was 'bollocks'. In 1987 we were still anticipating nuclear apocalypse, Sting was singing about 'Russians' and we'd never even met one. For some of us leather clad rebels it was Helter Skelter coming down fast, and our small bunch of nomadic road warriors would live off the bones of the old world.

Gone was the neat skinhead image of Fred Perry shirts, skin tight Levis and two-tone braces. It was oil-stained denim and leather, hair and beards that found their own style, psychedelic mushrooms and Newcastle Brown. In any case, we behaved like animals everywhere we went. We were the Mad Mile Club of the A20 corridor and we didn't give a shit what anybody thought.

There was this woman called Laura, who looked to be in her late thirties, a hippy type with big hair and sunglasses that hid half of her face. She looked good in faded denim and smoky pub lighting – well that's what I thought when I met her at a band night down the Duck. She used to turn up some places with her sixteen year old daughter Sara and they had both just come back from one of the Arabian

Gulf states, giving the impression (to us who'd never been anywhere) that they were some kind of bohemians.

Laura had invited us: that was me, Dave, Tony, Martin and Big John Landers (AKA Snowbeast) to a party at her house on the edge of Lyminge forest. It was a cold night in December and we all went on bikes. It was supposed to be a laid back, do as you like, mellow affair with beanbag furniture and marijuana music.

We went wild. This bloke called Chris (one of Laura's good friends) started it off by saying 'Do you want to see my party trick' and head-butting a plate of sardines. Sara was out of her head on something; she came over and kissed me, then tried to crack a bottle over my head, screamed and fell on the floor. Tony was going through the underwear in some kind of airing cupboard, after having raided the larder and eaten the middle out of two loaves of bread. I think Dave was collapsing some furniture when Laura freaked out, hurling a wooden stool through a doorway and across the kitchen, where a leg broke off it.

The place was a mess, there was food thrown everywhere and Chris led the host upstairs to calm her down, for an hour. With the lights on it didn't look pretty; there were boot marks part way up the wall, the bathroom was covered in horse mash and when someone refilled the kettle after having made us all a cup of tea, they found the lump of coal that had turned the water green.

I for one felt guilty, and when Chris came back downstairs he organised a clean up. It took half the night, including a frosty foray into the forest in search of a suitable Christmas tree, which we then decorated for Laura. She was fine in the morning, but I don't remember we saw much of her after that.

I was working pretty much full time for my dad by this

time, doing a multitude of stuff for his various endeavours: farming, commercial fishing, mechanics and building. I still spent a lot of my own time keeping junked vehicles on the road, it was my obsession. See below, a bunch of diary entries recorded verbatim:

### Thursday 10th December
'My birthday, I took off the old rusty bumper from my Datsun & welded up a new one nice and strong.'

### Friday 11th December
'I went to the Duck with Chip & Martin – I went up the bank, hit a tree & rolled my Datsun onto its side coming back.'

### Thursday 17th December
'I have got the lights working on my car but not fixed down.'

### Friday 18th December
'I worked from 10.30 to 2.30 then an hour & half on my garage, took one wall down & rebuilt it cause it was wrong. Then I spent till 10 pm welding my car back at the farm & slept on the front room floor with the dogs.'

### Saturday 19th December
'I was glueing & welding til about 3pm then I took it over to Martin's for Armageddon painting. a mixture of matt black, pot black, bitumen black, varnish, cement powder, coal dust & thinners. It looks the part now.'

That crash, after only three weeks of owning the car, was the best crash I've ever had. I was coming up Stone Hill, back towards Sellindge and didn't anticipate the sharpness of the bend. I went straight up the steep bank, swung it back down onto the road and went up the opposite bank, back down onto the road and right up the first bank again, until I hit a tree at the top. The car came down off the bank and settled on its side in the road. I unbuckled myself and climbed out of the passenger door unhurt.

I realised that there was a car stopped further up the hill with its lights on me. People had got out and were shouting that there was petrol running down the road. They wouldn't come down and help me though, just waited at a safe distance while I pushed the Datsun back over onto its wheels. I got in and drove it back to Kestrels.

The near side front wing was all crushed in and fouling the front wheel but I'd got her home that night, and over to the farm the next morning. I put quite a lot of work into fixing her up, and she came out of it a whole new shape. I'd welded an old headlamp into the reconstructed void and a strip of steel skirting at the front, below where the bumper had been. A box section steel frame made up the front line and I welded two small grills (from the back of a fridge) onto this at each end to cover the headlights. I glued up the broken indicators and the rear light cluster that had been smashed, using bits of broken light cover from other scrap vehicles we had on the farm. The bodywork was evened out using hammers and levers, it looked like screwed up newspaper that had been smoothed out again.

The paint job was inspired, it made the car look as if it had come straight out of a *Mad Max* film; I drove it like it had too. Years of being run into the gutter on my bikes, by cars coming and going from the Black Horse pub had made me a little bitter. I didn't slow down, or give way to anyone on my road and I always won a game of chicken. I even ran Woody off the road once, 'cause I didn't know it was him 'til it was too late. I did go back to apologise, then my starter motor wouldn't kick back in. So Woody gave me a bump start, using his own car to shunt me forward fast enough to do the job.

I'd always liked Woody; it had been him and Phil that I always got in trouble with out of school when we were kids, on our bicycles, climbing peoples' conker trees and rummaging through the dumps, looking for old pram wheels to make go-carts with.

More diary entries:

**Thursday 21st January 1988**
'It was frosty this morning & I hacked it round the T-junction in Moorstock Lane & slid into the hedge hitting a tree but doing no real damage thanks to my front grid.'

**Friday 18th March**
'My car has just about had it I think, with only 2nd, 4th & reverse and a chronic clutch slip.'

**Monday 21st March**
'I know why I have lost 2 gears, its cause my engine is dropping out of the frame & pulling on the gear stick.'

**Thursday 24th March**
'My day off, Will & Dell came over, we fitted the exhausts on my KH & Triumph & welded up my car chassey to the engine mounts.'

**Saturday 28th May**
'I fixed my Datsun exhaust again with a bit of copper piping & carted a few more slabs over, everyone looks at my car now I have wired a set of cow horns to the front.'

The Datsun came to rest later that summer after the fuel

pump gave out. I rigged up a gravity feed with a motorcycle fuel tank strapped to the bonnet which worked alright but it didn't have much range. However I left the car parked in the field for a while with the handbrake on and found the brakes had seized up solid. No amount of hammering or towing it around would shake them loose, so I abandoned the old thing.

Life was moving on, I was working most days and saving some money. I was generally staying out of the pubs weeknights. I won't say I was becoming more responsible, just rather more aware of bigger things, and it was all outside the village. I knew there was stuff out there in the world to experience, but I didn't yet know how to find it. I had some theories and I was reading more and more books; I was going to become a religious nutter, or a soldier of fortune, something along those lines.

# CHAPTER 4: NEW AGE TRAVELLERS

Dad said I could build a barn in the back field, out of telegraph poles and corrugated iron. I spent most of my spare time that summer and autumn constructing a fortress; it wasn't actually finished until the following summer, with doors hung, locks fitted and a storage loft added. I did it largely by my own hands, splitting poles with a circular saw, axes, hammers and wedges. Once the 30 ft timbers were prepared, I raised them using ropes and ladders, then used a brace and bit to drill the holes, before club-hammering the long bolts home. It was hard work, not to mention the digging by hand of twenty one four foot post holes through flint and clay. Cladding the structure in tin and then tar-painting it all took about a month in itself.

The plan was to use most of it for storing tractors and equipment, leaving just one section in the centre for me to convert into a place I could live in. I needed a Rayburn for cooking and heating and went to buy an old one from a bloke called Les, a biker and vintage car restorer who lived next to Sean Lincoln on Swan Lane.

Sean was our Essex boy racer, who had come to the village a couple of years previously; he was a townie really, but we got on with him alright. When I went to look at the Rayburn, Sean was outside on the road in his Gyppo vest, filling some holes in the front of a Transit van. I got talking and it turned out he wanted £150 for the Tranny, a 1600 MK2. I offered £120, so Sean said 'I'll toss you for it'. The coin went up and the Rayburn went in the back of my new van. Within days I was beating out sheet steel to weld strips and patches where they were needed around the lower sections. The top two thirds of the shell was in good condition so I left that blue, I painted all the base section with the same bitumen tar paint I was using for my corrugated iron. Later I constructed a very solid bumper and front bars out of thick box section steel, with more fridge grills; this bull bar wrapped around the nose of the van, giving it the look of a riot bus.

My driving became more careless in this new wagon and I had several minor scrapes in that van. Martin had moved into a caravan at a farmhouse outside Ashford and I was heading over there. The lanes were narrow but usually empty and I swung it round a bend, where I met a car head-on. There would have been just enough road width to pass, but the other car just stopped dead in the middle of the road. I put my foot down and went up the bank – if that car had kept moving it would have been okay, but I had no choice other than swing it back down onto the road. I slammed against the rear of the car, forcing a way through and, sorry to say, I just kept driving. My bumper wasn't even bent when I checked it over for damage at Martin's.

There were two caravans sited there and it became quite a meeting place for bearded types. When one old boy was found dead there the following summer, Chip moved in to his shabby caravan. It didn't even get redecorated and no one wanted to sit in there with him, but everyone hung out at Martin's anyway.

My van was often used as a troop carrier on party nights. I could get everyone in who wanted to come. One night before Christmas 88, we had a party planned. Actually it was a girl across the road from Kestrels, Carol Rolf, who was supposed to be having a birthday party, it kind of suited, as her birthday was the day before mine and I hadn't thought to do anything. We had built her a bonfire down the brook in Corner Wood and we got the van stuck in the bottom field hauling pallets and stuff down there. Carol had some problem on the night and never made it to her party, but we did.

A full session at the Dukes was followed by a load of us making it back to Kestrels with hoppers of beer to get the van and the mushroom dust. With everyone aboard I set off down the driveway and crashed straight into one of the brick pillars Rodger had built at the gateway. It went over in one piece separated from the base, so we just stood it upright again, hoped Rodger wouldn't notice and headed off down to the brook.

We were loaded up with extra pallets, waste fuel and a shredded tyre that had come off the van earlier. I'd driven it flat, halfway back from Tonbridge, in the rain. If you keep your speed up you can still drive on a flat, but once you start cornering and shredding the walls you've had it. We started the fire with this thing, stuffed with newspaper and dowsed in oil. The party had begun.

There were fireworks and there was stupidity, then torchlight coming across the field. It got closer and started to light up the edge of the woodland. I marched off to see what was going on and stumbled straight into the face of Kent Police. Fortunately it was Dave Bates, the village bobby, sent out to investigate a firearms incident. He knew me quite well and, convinced it was just harmless fun, he let me off with a warning. I told him we would be winding it all up soon and we were out of fireworks too by that time, so that was that. I went back to the fire site and it was deserted. There was just a portable hi-fi sitting there with hippy music flowing through the trees in an empty wood. I wasn't going to try driving out of there, so just settled down by the fire to see my own birthday in with the dawn.

We had two or three other bonfire parties down there over the next few years. One was fancy dress; that was when Heapsy piled the fire up so high in pyromaniac frenzy that the leaves of the big old oak tree got scorched. I was dressed as a Viking, with an outfit hurriedly made from old coal sacks and ancient carpet underlay. I had a tin helmet that was really an old headlamp shell, stuffed with a moth eaten fox skin that I got banned from wearing in the pub.

The best one was probably when I got second degree burns across my lower back and buttocks. We played this game called 'burn the people alive': you had to climb out along a horizontal branch of the old oak, 'til you were over the fire. Then waste oil would be thrown into the fire to cause a flame-up. If you could hang in there you passed the test. I was clowning around on the branch and fell onto the pile. I was so drunk, I didn't bother trying to get off it until I could feel the searing heat coming through my jacket. Hedges insisted on driving me into William Harvey hospital, so a car load of us went in. My clothes, hair and beard were all singed and I had been dowsed in beer and Pernod, then rolled around in the swampy brook for good measure. What we must have looked like walking into casualty! When I came out of the treatment room, wrapped in a Freddy Mercury style string vest and trunks, I didn't see Hedges; they told me he was having his stomach pumped. A little while later a nurse pushed him out in a wheel chair. He was whimpering and had vomit all down his front. Some other joker who reckoned they were fit to drive took charge of the wheels for the ride back.

During that winter after Carol's party, Tone and I

prepared the van for a road trip to the Isle of Wight – don't know why we chose February. We cleaned the plugs, fixed the rear lights, changed the points condenser set and then had a go at sorting out the leaky radiator, with Radweld and raw eggs.

More diary entries:

**Friday 10th February**
'Me and Tony left in the Transit for the Isle of White. The exhaust back box fell off in my hands at a roadside burger stop. We went to see the Mary Rose & the HMS Victory then got over the water. Non-stop rock music took us through to dusk where the tires were screeching around the bends in the country road to Tolland Bay. The pubs were unimpressive. We parked down on the sea wall.'

The exhaust had been damaged on the way off the farm; the new track-way to the barn had been hastily laid with piles of dumped kerb-stones and broken rubble. I got Chip, Martin and a bunch of Hythe bikers to help me do it in the summer: it almost broke us. Parts of this track still resembled the Giants Causeway and I had reversed into a block sticking out, thus bending the rear part of my exhaust system back on itself. And yes, I do remember nearly wiping out as we came into a sudden bend on that road to Tolland. Queen was blaring out from the tape player and we were singing along to 'Don't Stop Me Now', we got to the bit where it goes 'I'm travelling at the speed of light' just as we hit the bend and it would have been wrong to touch the brakes.

That Saturday morning was clear and bright; the sun coming through the big windscreen while we drove along the southern coast road from Freshwater made it feel like spring. I was shirtless in the cab, rocking to 'Free Bird': it felt like I was driving along the edge of the world and we might never come back.

We were on the mainland that same afternoon actually, and driving through the New Forest. We made camp at the Rufus Stone, a small memorial to William the Second (who was killed with an arrow shot by Walter Tyrrell whilst out hunting). We had a beer in the pub there and one of the locals said we should make it over to the Coach and Horses at Cadnam, just outside Southampton. They weren't wrong, there was a great band playing at the pub, called Reggie and the Mounties. It was all acoustic instruments, harmonica and ukuleli, no amp. Everyone thought they were a joke band to start with, but they were really very smart and entertained the rowdy crowd all evening. There was country music and lots of Everly Brothers classics. 'Knees Up Mother Brown' had all the inbreds kicking up their heels and the band took the piss out of us as much as we thought we were laughing at them.

It rained a little that night, but we got off the grass alright the next morning. Those short wheelbase Transits were hopeless on soft ground because they were only single wheel axels and they were worse empty than they were with a load on. We spent the Sunday cruising around and ended up at Hurst Castle, right at the end of a one and a half mile shingle bank, with sea on one side and tidal lagoons on the other.

On our way back up through the forest, we were flagged down by a nicely turned out coloured girl in a denim mini skirt. She ran up to the door and was in before we had a chance to ask where she was going. She smiled at me, a big wide grin that showed off her rotted black teeth, then told us she had bunked off from a drug rehab centre and would

43

us 'nice boys' like to take her to London. We dropped her off three miles down the road at Brockenhurst train station, then made it back to the Dukes for the evening session.

The following weekend was my housewarming party at the barn I had built. I hadn't sorted out doors at this point, so the whole front was open. We hung a giant dusty tarpaulin from the top beam. Tony and I had found it down at the West Hythe canal, all covered in wet clay.

The floor of my new home was the Earth's crust and the only furniture in there was a picnic bench I'd stolen from the beer garden at the Dukes; after a drunken night at the pub I'd walked it back along the main road to Kestrels, on my back, like a tortoise. I actually sold that same bench the following year to the new land lord of the Mucky Duck: I got twenty five quid, which everyone thought was quite funny.

My van did the pub crawl with the Dukes Head faithful that evening: Tony, Derek, Keebles, Tritton and Chip. We did the Tiger, Five Bells, Blue Anchor (re-christened the Blue Oyster Bar) and the Dukes Head again. The drive over there was manic and I skidded it all the way round my track to crash through my own field gate. We cooked and ate two chickens and Neil made a brew with the last of his dried magic mushrooms. Martin and Greasy Colin turned up late and beer started to fly. I came out with a crate of Guinness that I'd found under one of the scrap piles when clearing the land to build the barn. It had been outside for at least ten years and the tops of the bottles were just rust scabs. We were just smacking the necks off them against farm machinery to swig back the foul dregs. I have never appreciated the praise everyone has for Guinness – I've tried it two or three times since then to prove a point and I still can't stand it. That night turned into a crazed mêlée, where we were chasing each other around with broken bottles full of rancid ale. We looked like drowned rats at the end of it. I can still hear the bursts of laughter and the tape player throwing out 'We Came Here To Rock!'

I actually didn't have to sleep in the open barn, as it was. Dad had bought a little painted wooden living-wagon from a traveller family at Whitstable and we'd pushed it under the front of the barn, next door to my section. It was tiny, with a bunk-bed, two slim wall cupboards and a chest of drawers. I put an old travelling trunk under the bunk and a mantelpiece clock on the front step. My lighting was just candles; my heating came from the old cast iron 'Queenie' stove. I had a bucket of water for washing and a Primus stove for boiling water. The only power I had was from a car battery that I wired up to a stereo from one of the scrap cars. I had a song book, a harmonica and my old school recorder. I never spent more contented evenings anywhere in the world from that day to this.

That Transit van was like a right of passage for me, but I had no right to drive it the way I did. It brought out in me the worst road sense, but I had the most fun in it and I just didn't care. I felt untouchable; it was down to other people on the road to see me coming. Now I hate that kind of attitude when I see it out there, and I hate the people who behave in the way I did. Growing up isn't straight forward and for some young men there comes a period in life when it doesn't seem to be wrong to just say 'What the fuck!'

Sometimes not giving a shit was genuinely funny; I'd just driven up the front drive to my mum and dad's place and parked at the top, in front of the garage workshop, I was out for a minute or two, then got back into the drivers' seat. I whacked it into reverse and went for the three point turn. The resulting crash surprised me somewhat, and when

I got out, I saw that some idiot had parked a new F reg. car in my blind spot – my blind spot being pretty much anywhere within thirty feet of my rear doors. I had to go into the house to hand out the bad news and ironically; the car belonged to an insurance salesman who had just turned up. Fair exchange no robbery.

That Easter, I took the van off on my own road trip to Cornwall, with a KT250 trial bike in the back for company. I had planned to be away for four weeks and my first stop was the Coach and Horses at Cadnam. There I saw a poster advertising Reggie and the Mounties back to play on the Saturday week. Well that decided it, I finished my beer and got back into the driving seat; I would get to Lands End and back to this pub inside one week, a whistle-stop tour.

My life has always been a series of well laid plans, interjected by stabs of shear impulse. The following morning, I was driving across Dartmoor, swigging from a keg of scrumpy and singing along to 'Sweet Home Alabama'. I took a wing mirror out against a dry stone wall on the downhill section into Tavistock.

**Diary entry for Saturday 25th March**
'I drove right across Dartmoor & into Cornwall by the Packhorse Bridge at 12.30. I went to Castle An Dinas (hill fort) & Roche Rock, then past Truro & through Penryn then I went into the back of a parked car on the outskirts of Falmouth. I then took a more leisurely drive around the Helford river, to Lizard point & had a Cornish pasty.'

I can't believe how many stops I made during that week as I toured the peninsular, but looking back in the old diary it seems I didn't miss much out. I was sleeping in the back of the van each night and washing in the sea. When I could, I read books by candle light and played my harmonica often.

One pub I ended up in, at St Agnes late one night, had me chatting with an ex-Royal Marine who was into extreme kayaking. I had recently been learning to dive, so we had some relative connection. A few years after that, Derek and I did actually canoe along the Military Canal in Kent, most of the way to Rye, but that was it. An ambition I developed to canoe across to the Isles of Scilly never materialised though and I let that one go. Just as well really.

More diary entries:

### Friday 31st March

'I got the KT out & set off over Rough Tor to find 'King Arthur's Hall', I found it (just a rectangular setting of some granite rocks in the middle of miles of boggy moorland). I went on and got to the tarmac at Jamaica Inn right in the middle of Bodmin Moor. I had three halfs and a pasty. Then I rode through Altarnum & cut across the moors back to Rough Tor. I almost got stuck fast in bog at the accumulation for the de lank river. I steamed up the tor & back down to the van, covered in wet peat. The day was now hot so I did 50 minutes sunbathing & drove through Launceston, past Okenhampton, Exeter, Taunton & stopped off at Glastonbury Tor.'

### Sunday 2nd April

'I picked up a complete Ford Escort exhaust from the layby that I stopped at outside Eastbourne. When I got back I tidied my van & caravan & did my washing up. I went to the Dukes & then we all went back to Kestrals (now Derek's place) for a piss up. Warren dived through the serving hatch into the back of the TV.'

The summer of 89 was a golden season for me, as well as the beginning of a transition. I thought I was starting to develop into someone and I knew I was going to make something of my life, but hadn't worked out what. I had strong views on various subjects, but they were conflicting. I worked from dawn to dusk on the farm, which Dad had developed into an activity and training centre for an alternative to custody program. My job had mostly become teaching motorcycle mechanics and trials riding skills, as well as managing most of the farm maintenance.

We had a multitude of staff members come and go, including Volkswagen enthusiast 'Stanhope' Steve, Neil Smith (who used to run A1 Bike Breakers) and not forgetting Wayne Gifford: he was from a farming family up on the hill. Wayne had recently come back from an Israeli Kibbutz, done the 'Grand Tour' and taken the famed 'Magic Bus' back through Europe. I picked up tips from all of these people, and more, during that period where I was trying to decide what path my life would take.

I was still getting banned regularly from all the local pubs, but as they seemed to change hands every couple of years there were always one or two I could get into and still have a laugh in. The Dukes Head set were the most solid and we generally all got on. The Duck was used for band nights and beer throwing. It had its own set of regulars based around Chris Woods and his sports biker mates. We had nicknames for them all: Christopher Woodruff key, Daddy Longlegs, Tash Rash and Fish Eyes were the ones I can remember.

Hythe people tended to get out to the Duck and Ashford people to the Dukes, the East/West divide. The Black Horse and the Five Bells also had band nights and they were neutral territory, both being out of the way venues you had to drive to and mostly drawing in the more townie crowds.

Drinking and driving just didn't seem to bother people then, no one ever called the police as we were all at it. To my knowledge, only Martin ever got breathalysed and banned; that only happened because he had a pretty bad crash on an evil chopper he had built himself.

I got invited to a couple of Oakmen parties that summer, Martin and I turned up to one of them at Bethersden village hall in the Transit. We spent the night drinking with Chip and 'Sick George' – there was something wrong with that man. We took it in turns driving back to the caravan at Sevington, along a route which seemed to be all trees and corners. Raging on speed and the Anti Nowhere League, it was a wonder we got back at all.

I used to like getting up with a band that regularly played at the Duck, called 'Fantasia'. They were sort of post-hippy/early Punk Rock. I would do the ANL version of 'Streets of London', a bit of softer stuff like 'Crying in the Rain', some Johnny Cash and then that ANL classic 'Woman'. It starts off all soothing and tender about love and respect, then half way through it climbs into full-on, really offensive Punk Rock, full of hatred and disgust. It was brilliant.

Diary entries:

**Friday 21st July 1989**
'After work I put away all my things, locked up & packed my bags, picked up Tony & David (Keeble) & we drove off for Somerset. We stopped in Swindon, very big town & had a drink at a rebel biker type pub, then a tenners worth of fried chicken. We drove to Lydington & it was so hot we were lying on the van roof at 11 or 12 o'clock listening to Tony's tape player.'

## Saturday 22ⁿᵈ July

'We found Badbury hill fort, reputed to be Mount Baddon where King Arthur slaughtered the Saxons, then we took an old disused road from Badbury Castle on the Ridgeway, five miles to Marlborough, that was worse than Keebles' track. A dusty laugh though, loose cassette tapes bouncing around on the dash, we lost one through a hole in the door well. We stopped at Avebury village for a drink and to have a look around at the stone circles. Then on to Glastonbury. There was a sweet girl at a roadside service park who I kept buying cups of tea from. At Glastonbury I had my horoscope calculated by an old druid type in an immaculate wooden wagon at the foot of the hill. Everything he said about me was remarkably accurate. We had a bit of an adventure up on the Tor that night.'

That evening on Glastonbury Tor was one not to be forgotten. We'd spent the afternoon in the town, looking like road trash ourselves, but still scornful of the 'new age travellers' and peace convoy scum (that's how I saw them). My younger sister Ann had recently turned vegan and gone off with some to lose herself. I hated that set: they turned everything that had been beautiful about the hippy movement and grunged it all up. They hated the system but sponged off the state and resented anyone who had worked to earn their own piece of England. The hippies had had the Vietnam War to protest about; this lot thought society was unfair because of the poll tax. All that aside, my little sister and I had more in common than we would ever admit to.

That early evening in high summer, three friends set off to climb the hill. Meeting the astrologer (who probably wasn't that old really) had touched something in me which hung in tight well into my twenties. I still see astrology as a science instead of a superstition. So with packets of crisps, cans of drink and some oranges, we staked out our plot on the western side of the tor. I opened my 'snuff box' which was actually an empty container for .22 starter pistol blanks. We shared out the last of the mushroom dust and waited, as we watched the sun set over the town and the Somerset Levels.

There were some weird looking people up there, amongst the regular types, but we forgot about them as we settled into our trip. A young girl, hands palms up resting on her knees, let out a series of long high notes as the sun disappeared; we thought that was quite a strange thing to do.

Nothing happened for a long time, then the stars came out and clouds began to take on shapes. At first it was an incredible experience, lying back at the top of the most spiritual point in the whole of southern England. I could see straight lines (leys) reaching out to other high points on the landscape and I felt my mind guided like it was locked into a telegraph network to other places; churches, mounds, stones and even the pyramids of Egypt and Mexico. I felt I had stumbled upon the answer, the whole reason for my life up to that point. One of the images I saw in the clouds was of the Earth Goddess.

We noticed firework displays some miles from us in opposite directions, then a dozen aircraft flew over us like a squadron of bombers. Other people on the mound were exclaiming surprise at the lights in the sky so I know that happened. I thought of the Russians, the Martians and then it occurred that it may be the men from Atlantis, homing in on the Earth transmitter, the Tor.

An apparently normal couple, a bit older than us, came over and we chatted about what was going on. They weren't weirdos, so we relaxed and were laughing and joking about with them. Then another squadron flew over and I realised

51

that people were appearing all over the crown of the hill, I thought they were frightened hippies emerging to seek sanctuary up high or hoping maybe to be evacuated by Atlanteans. Maybe it was the end of the world and the lights had been an early warning signal to the enlightened and not a firework display at all.

Right then I was starting to wonder if I'd been wrong and that maybe hippies and new age travellers might actually be 'the meek who would inherit the earth'. A couple of really scruffy young blokes, who looked like they slept in a dog kennel, came up and joined us and I remember having seen them playing the bongos, down below earlier in the day. They talked about earth and how they were 'into dirt', we could see it was all over them and laughed. It was odd that they seemed to be familiar with the first couple who had befriended us; you wouldn't have guessed, by their appearances that there would be any connection. What was even weirder was that the first couple didn't seem at all concerned about what was going on behind us: the fact that all over the top of the hill there were marauding spaced out sub-humans. What the hell were they doing?

The woman went off to the ruined church on the level space behind us; I saw her go in, then shortly after, she came back out wrapped in a black cloak. The wind took it as she walked towards us, revealing that she was naked beneath it. That alarmed me, she was good looking okay, but no matter, I was feeling quite nervous and I hadn't signed up for some black magic ritual. I tried hinting at the others that it was time to go, but they weren't understanding why and I didn't want to break the calm.

I knew it couldn't be right, that people en mass would leave the pubs down below at 11.30 and all make their way up here. I voiced curiosity more than once and the woman in black said 'Oh there's a lot more of us than you'd imagine who come up here.' It was a bit of a *Hammer House of Horror* moment. The thought dawned on me that they did have a motive for befriending us earlier on. Clearly everyone around us was a member of some Devil worshiping cult and I'll admit I started to freak out a bit. I'd taken more mushroom dust than the other two, but all the same I was convinced that we were going to be the subject of an initiation ceremony of some kind. I'd seen enough horror films to know that someone usually has to die. The two scruffy blokes didn't seem like peace loving earth children anymore, while the first couple just said 'Stay, it's alright' but no-one was explaining anything.

Almost certainly at midnight, probably thirteen people all dressed in grey cloaks and hoods filed out of the old ruin. That was it for me and I stood up, making a bit of a scene actually. David looked worried, but Tony was oblivious as usual. He lost a button from his new stereo set in the scramble to get us going. Paranoid as I may have been, I knew that whole thing wasn't right and told them, 'Fucking walk, right now!' and I made us march off that hill followed by laughter and chants of 'You'll never get off the mound' and 'They won't get to the bottom.'

My feet were slow and my shoulder bag was getting incredibly heavy. It felt as if the hill possessed a magnetism that was preventing us from moving away from its centre. It was also growing taller and steeper, so that I could see we wouldn't be able to reach the bottom. We stopped part-way along the zigzag trail and stepped off it onto the hillside. There I opened my bag – and a lock knife I was carrying. I dumped all the food and drink out for some reason, but not the oranges. I ate two whole, skins and all, as if they were apples. I needed to come down and the vitamin C would help. The can of Tizer probably would have helped too but it was sitting on the hillside, too heavy to carry and no one was going back for it. We seemed to be getting somewhere at last but paused at the base of the hill where we had to gather some determination to make it through the trees to the road below. We did it, and I was standing in the middle of the road, eating another whole orange, when a police car pulled up and one of the cops asked 'Everything okay?' Without thinking I replied 'Not really, there's some strange people up there.' Instantly I wished I hadn't said it, as I felt that chill feeling down the back of my neck and he said 'Oh there's a lot of strange people in this town.' After a bit of questioning they let us on our way. I'd said we just wanted to get to our van and drive, and we never wanted to come back. I probably shouldn't have mentioned the van either, as I shouldn't have been driving, but we weren't going to be sitting parked up under that hill all night.

As we walked up to the van, Dave admitted that he was 'terrified', Tone seemed not to have been much affected. My mind gradually became steady: those oranges had done the job. We found the van, standing bravely in the National Trust car park where we had left it, there was no sign of anyone lurking. We could hear some kind of ritualistic howls coming from somewhere up on the mound. We approached the van cautiously, then I was in and Tone was under the bonnet with the easy start, while David kept a look-out. It took a few turns of the key, but then fired, and we were away and moving, through the collection of hippy wagons, there were quite a few other cars there, new executive type vehicles (not the sort that hippies would drive). They stood out from the rest of the dross, reinforcing the belief that what was going on up on the hill was not an accidental gathering of spiritualists.

We drove out of Glastonbury, a few miles to the nearest range of hills, and finally began to laugh a little about the whole thing. Tone went to sleep and Dave and I stayed up in the back, drinking tea, until there was a knock on the back doors at 3 am! This had us scrambling for weapons; we had a bayonet I'd bought that day from an antiques shop and the chopping axe to hand. I opened the doors. It was some young bloke saying he had run out of petrol, and did we have any? Well we did but I said 'No.' Then he asked if we had any engine oil and he got the same response. We didn't fancy being turned into a sacrifice bonfire while we slept, by some crazed occultist group. It was probably a freak encounter, but a bloody odd one and bad timing to say the least. I got back in the driver's seat and put a few more miles between us and that hill. More cups of tea followed and we finally crashed out sometime before sunrise.

It was some drive back to Sellindge, A roads all the way, and Dave had to take the wheel after I actually fell asleep on the A27 Lewis to Eastbourne road. We had all zoned out and the first I knew was that David had grabbed the wheel out of my hands and we were bumping along, two wheels on the grass verge, I snapped out of it and let him drive for the rest of the way. Tony was crashed out in the back and never woke up at all.

I had two more accidents in the Transit that summer; one when I was working at Warehorne for the Taylor-Lowens', sorting, dismantling and re-fitting old church pews for pubs and restaurants mainly. Reversing up past one of the small workshops, I caught the rear door and wing of a newish looking Orion that was parked on the edge of the driveway. It was the claw of my front light grill that did it. I say 'caught', but clearly I scraped along a good few feet of it. There was nothing for it but to go and own up, the poor bloke was just there to choose a church pew and I don't think he bought one. When I led him back down the drive to view the scene, he asked if it was badly damaged. I said 'Depends what you call *badly*.' Just at that point we were rounding the corner and the car came into view. 'That's badly!' he said.

This next diary entry recorded my forth shunt of that summer:

**Friday 18ᵗʰ August**

'I drove my van to Crowhurst & Toad took me round some bloke's house to buy a load of KH250 bits. I went back to Ashford to draw out bike money & got into a parking difficulty by the tattooists. I reversed into a Capri who hadn't seen me, I had to give details.'

By this stage in my driving career I could genuinely see the value of a third party insurance policy. Breakdown insurance, with recovery, was also going to be money well spent in the not to distant future. All that would have to wait until the new year though, as Wayne had enthused me with his tales of travelling East on a shoe-string budget and I was off to Israel. Firstly to work on a Kibbutz for three months, I'd meet people and see a bit of the world. It would do something for me: just the jolt I needed.

# CHAPTER 5: THE BEDFORD CHALLENGE

**Diary entry Friday 20th April 1990**
'I managed to smash the front of Dad's new Toyota Tercel a little today, not good really. I went up the Dukes, broke a stool, that's about it.'

I was back in the routine, and still not looking where I was going. That did cause a bit of an upset, it might even have been the first time I'd driven the Toyota; it wasn't new, but it was clean enough to call it that.

**Diary entry Saturday 19th May 1990**
'I worked 4 hours for Keebles at £4 per hr. Did some floor levelling in my barn & picked up the Bedford from Don, very strange to drive. I went up the Dukes, Chip was up there & Del & Sue his cute new girlfriend. I paid my bar bill in 117 and a half pennies just to rile Pat behind the bar & it worked. Sue couldn't stop laughing, I'd been saving those pennies for years.'

The pale blue Bedford HA van I bought for £75 was probably the worst car I've owned. Harry and Sean from when I worked on the council had driven around in a bright yellow one with the confederate flag painted on the bonnet and *Dukes of Hazard* air horns. Mine didn't really have any style. I had some fun with it though. The weekend next was Whitsun bank holiday and the Sellindge Steam

Rally; I got my mate Alan from Gravesend to come over for the weekend.

Alan and I had been best mates at Kibbutz Ramot Menashe; he had worked in the Aram, a mini factory where they revamped water meters that looked just like Aladdin's lamps. He did have a bit of a drinking issue and when we were out there, we held regular drinking parties down in the volunteer quarters on the edge of the site that everyone called 'the Ghetto'. Just before I left the Kibbutz, we prepared a big bonfire party, with wood we had been dragging up from the dump all week in readiness for the Friday night Shabbat. When all the guests (mostly South Americans) had left, it had just been the two of us out there and we scoured the site for more fuel. We burned anything we could find and actually dragged out two beds from one of the unoccupied rooms to throw on. Gabi, the Volunteer manager, turned up when the fire was at its height and asked us where we had got all the wood. We went on 'til dawn and Alan even burned his own mattress. I burned my work boots.

Back to the Steam Rally now. There was always a Saturday night party in the beer tent for the traders and showmen, but it was free to turn up to and they had live music. It was usually a couple who played accordion melodies and I used to sing folk songs and sea shanties with them backing me, the oldies loved it, as did I. After the tent closed, I drove us the two miles back to the caravan and I thought the van was giving up: I had to rev it like mad and slip the clutch to get it out of the field. Once on the road I got it moving, but it was just getting slower and slower and I finished the drive in first gear. When I went out to have a look in the morning, I found that the handbrake had been on the whole time. That had almost certainly made for a safer than usual drive home.

Alan was great company, we'd sit on my caravan step drinking bottles of cheap wine and laughing about stuff while the sun went down beyond the wood. Whenever I had guests over they got the hospitality of the back of my old Transit, a rug and a candle, no pillow as I never used one myself then. Del used to call it 'Bedford and no breakfast'. The simple days were great, they cost nothing and you'd remember them for ever. Sometimes I would be driving along the country roads and just start laughing to the world about this ridiculous and outrageous lifestyle.

Half way through July that year I decided I was going to drive the Bedford to Scotland. I set off after 1am on Tuesday the seventeenth and I got pulled up before Maidstone for some reason. Then I drove 'til 4am, almost to Cambridge, with only a slight hint of trouble with the engine faltering a couple of times. I think most people would have turned around and come straight back home, but I had this belief in fate and purpose. I knew that I was meant to go to Scotland.

I stopped in Yorkshire to visit my Aunty Sue and Uncle Gary, it was the first time I'd ever been up there to see them. Gary took me down to his local for a pint of bitter and a chat with the regulars about golf and cricket and rural Yorkshire. It was not the sort of evening I was used to, but I quite enjoyed it. Those blokes were quite similar to my old mate Phil's dad Andy, who himself had come from mining stock at Aylesham in Kent. Entire mining communities had been relocated from Yorkshire a hundred years previously to work the coal mines down South and I think that's where Andy's militant socialist outlook came from too.

I had a good night's sleep on a very comfortable bed, with a pillow. I don't know why I didn't carry on with the habit: it couldn't have been so hard – unlike the back of a Bedford van, or my bed of wooden boards in the caravan.

I stopped next at Hadrian's Wall, which I mistakenly assumed was the border. Some time into the next day, when I passed a tartan-clad piper playing under a giant boulder with Scotland carved into, I knew I'd been wrong.

A couple of days later the van had settled in okay and I was camped by Urquhart Castle on the shore of Loch Ness, watching the dark still water for any hint of a phenomenon. Later that day I decided to head west to the Isle of Skye. I'd wanted to go there since I was about eight years old and we'd learned the Skye Boat Song at school. Also that's where my grandmother's Nicolson Tartan originated. I picked up a couple of European hitch-hikers along the way. They were pleasant enough company, but seemed a bit nervous about my driving, so they can't have been Italians. I soon realised that you can't just go up the bank to pass things in Scotland, because it's covered in big rocks and drainage furrows.

I loved Skye, the weather (on that occasion) was beautiful and the people were friendly. I wore rose tinted spectacles the whole way and obviously I was lucky on that trip. The Bedford started to tell me that it didn't much like the hills and the engine began dying out when it came under load. I thought it was probably the points failing, or the fuel system maybe. After a couple of days of driving round the island I picked up two German hitch-hikers and the extra weight proved too much so I had to dump them off short. I struggled on and coaxed that lump of metal back to the ferry point at Kyleakin, where it died on the entry ramp. The ferryman gave me a £3 refund and told me to buy a new car.

Once on the mainland, I stopped to check it over; no sooner had I got the lid open, then three Scotsmen in bonnets insisted on helping me to reset the points. It worked; I thanked them and was off and away to Fort William, where I parked up by the Caledonian Canal. I started from there in the mid morning, on a sudden impulse to get back home that same night. It was a tall order, I only stopped for petrol when I needed it, and once to eat a bowl of muesli while the engine cooled down. About 11.30 that night the motor died on me, I was on the M25 and it was the points. It happened again at the Dartford crossing barrier and I needed a push to get clear. I realised that the power was being drained by my tape player wired up to the battery, so probably the alternator was duff. I had to cut the headlights once I got onto the M20 for that long uphill crawl. The police stopped me and said it was illegal to drive on a motorway at night with only sidelights. I told them it couldn't do the hill with headlights on and asked for an escort, just to the top and I'd have been alright. They left me there on the hard shoulder, so I gave it twenty minutes in the dark and then fired up and carried on as I had been. I finally got home about 2am.

After recovering from my fourteen hour driving ordeal, I gave the van a service. I charged the battery up and rechecked the points. They were massively out again. I reset them and ran the engine, then I rechecked the gap. They were miles out! It transpired that my distributor had a bent central column; how that can occur I have no idea, but it meant that as the cam turned, the points gap could never stay correct and the thing was totally incapable of sparking most of the time. I got a second hand distributor centre for it, new plugs, points and condenser, but I stopped short of getting new leads and plug caps. I never did see how a circuit could fail, if wires are firmly connected to all components. Of course I know they do fail, but the van didn't justify any more than the most basic care and attention. I never loved that vehicle; not the colour, the wheels, the sound or the shape. The seats weren't even comfortable: it was just a thing to use.

The Bedford didn't have to last much longer, and it wasn't going to. Dave Keeble and I decided to take it out on a final trip (with AA breakdown cover) back to druid land to face our fears. We set off from the Dukes as usual and at Ashford I told Dave to put a tenner's worth of petrol in the tank. He got about £9.65 in there and then just kept the trigger down 'til the pump read £10.00. Petrol was spilling all down the side of the van and running onto the forecourt.

That trip didn't get much more sensible, as we drove into the night. The starter motor pushed itself out of the block and it seemed we'd lost two of the three bolts that should have secured it. We parked up at Bracknell and had a sleep in our seats, while the AA man got on with the job. In the early hours something else happened. Whilst bombing along the M4, only a few miles from our jumping off point, there was a sudden seizure. Then it broke free and you'd have thought there was a machine gun going off underneath, at about a thousand rounds a minute. It still drove, so I carried on to the next junction, where we turned off for Barbury Castle. By the time we found a suitable place to park up, the van was sounding more like the machine gun had had a silencer fitted. The place was an ancient earthworks, just off the Ridgeway track up on the Marlborough Downs, so we'd got somewhere at least.

In the morning we had a look underneath and it was clear what the problem was. The alloy casing that extended from the gearbox (it housed an oil seal and bearing presumably) had welded itself to the prop-shaft and sheared off an inch or so of aluminium from the main body. I couldn't see any oil spill, so clearly there was no oil in there. Anyway, the last five miles or so had rounded off the jagged faces and they had shrunk away from the break. There was no longer any contact worth talking about, just an undulating alloy ring stuck to the shaft.

We left the site by mid morning and took the five mile rough road that we knew about from the previous trip. It was a green lane I suppose, and sign-posted Marlborough, but looked like it got only agricultural traffic. I drove it like we'd entered a rally. It was the most fun I'd had on four wheels; noise, clouds of dust, the cassette player jumping around loose and us two laughing like banshees. I was pushing it to the edge rounding a curve, when we flew over a ramped up section and buried the front of the van into the bank like a rogue missile. We sat in silence for several moments while the dust cleared, then worked our way out of the crash and assessed the damage. The left wing was crunched, headlight gone, one front tyre burst and the brake line ripped out.

Most people would have said it was un-drivable, but not us boys. We had to jack it out of the bank, in order to get to the wheel and change it. We kicked, pulled and levered the twisted metal out of the way, so that the wheels would go round and we could move forward. The tracking was so wrecked that the two front wheels were at different angles and they churned up dust like a flour mill. Then, when we got it onto the tarmac, the tyres yelped and squealed all the way through the middle of Marlborough town. It was market day and we certainly drew some attention as we passed through the main square. It was about another eight miles to Avebury and I had to use force to hold the steering wheel straight all the way. It's a wonder the tyres held out, but I got it there and into the car park within the earth banks of the prehistoric site. Job done, we had a day at the stones and an evening at the local pub (the tiny village actually sits part within the banks of the circle); the locals must have thought we were just another couple of weirdos.

On the Sunday morning I phoned up the AA and we came back to Kent on the back of a recovery truck. Del and Tony just happened to be outside the Dukes Head as we came on through waving; you couldn't make it up if you tried.

# PART TWO
# REBELS WITH A CAUSE

# CHAPTER 6: ARMAGEDDON CAN WAIT

In September of 1990, I was offered another car, abandoned by Mr Taylor-Lowen's two daughters, in exchange for another day's work. It was a 1980 spec. Datsun Sunny estate, a 120 this time, and it had been custom painted by the two girls to look like a Friesian cow. This car was stronger and faster than the 100A had been; it was just the colour scheme that guaranteed you couldn't feel cool or hard driving it. I didn't like the car enough to make it my own really: it was just a slightly embarrassing work vehicle that was sure to make someone laugh any day I drove it. Another MOT failure, with only a month's tax on it this time.

The bastard broke down the very next week, as I drove it back from Hamstreet. I didn't quite make the uphill section just before Bilsington and I had to get it off the road before the fuzz came along. Luckily the starter motor alone got me to the crest of the hill, but I'd used up all the battery by constantly turning the ignition, forcing first gear to creep it forward to the nearest field entrance and I left it behind a hedge.

I hitched a lift to the 'Welcome Stranger' at Court-At-Street, and then ran the Harringe Lane stretch to get to Kestrels on the A20. From there I borrowed Del's pushbike to get to my place and load up a KH400 with tools, fuel and a spare battery. Taking Del on the back, I raced over to Bilsington and the car was still there undiscovered. We were able to fire her up and get ourselves back in time for a

Tuesday night out at the Duck. It was worth it, the Keeble brothers had a short punch-up in front of the fruit machine, while Fantasia played *Oliver's Army*, 'And I wouldn't rather be anywhere else but here today'.

I sold that car a year later, I never did attempt to tax, MOT or insure it; there didn't seem to be any point, as I avoided driving it into any towns. It was used mostly for carrying tools and materials around for gardening jobs I was doing. I sold it to Matt Godden, who'd just turned up in the village after a well deserved period of social exile. He said he'd sorted himself out and was looking for a cheap car to get him to Ashford and back. I think it was possibly his first ever job start. I won't say it was a good deal at £50, but it did get him started. I don't think he had it long and I know he never re-registered it in his name, so I suppose it was par for the course that the first time it broke down on him, his response was to set fire to it where it stood.

One day at Warehorne, I was cleaning out rubbish from the sheds and burning bits of old church pew wood for the Taylor-Lowens. As I stood around the bonfire stoking it, I noticed a bible starting to burn. I rescued it of course and it was open at Revelation, chapter seventeen, the Apocalypse of John. It was all about the Whore of Babylon, the Mother of Harlots and the Abominations of the Earth. Yes, we were approaching the end of days and I had a book to prove it. I'd been reading Nostradamus' predictions about the end of the world and by the end of the 80s, it had all seemed to be falling into play:

C2 Q89 - 'One day the great powers will become friends. The two will not remain allied for long. There will be such a loss on both sides, that one will bless Petrus Romanus (the end of millennium Pope).'

C2 Q62 - 'Mabus will soon die, then will come a horrible

slaughter of people and animals, at once vengeance is revealed coming from a hundred lands. Thirst, and famine when the comet will pass.'

Then there was the blood plague:

C3 Q75 – 'Swords damp with blood from distant lands. A very great plague will come with a great scab. Relief near but the remedies far away.'

Well it all happened, in moderation; by the end of the millennium we should have been living in a world on very different terms. I won't say I was disappointed by the anti-climax, but I reckon I would have taken a more responsible approach to life if Armageddon had not been on the cards. I had become a kind of survivalist in more ways than one; if it was all coming down, then I was getting prepared by hoarding petrol, water, bullets, tinned food and condoms. A lot of these things had degraded long before the millennium and my cache became as obsolete as Dudley's nuclear fall out shelter, or a Blue Peter time capsule; the whole end of days thing was just another casualty of the 20th century.

I used to make a trip into the old Ashford market every Saturday morning and fill an army backpack with dented tins and packets of dry food. In the evenings I would sit in the little wooden caravan, drinking tea and eating shortbread and salted peanuts by candle light. I had a donkey called Jake (who ate tea bags) and a black cat that would come and sit on the platform at the top of the wooden steps every evening and wait for me to give him some dinner. A chicken used to nest in a coil of barbed wire just under the front of the wagon and lay me an egg for my breakfast most mornings. One night there was a terrible squawking and flapping and I was up and out like a flash to see a badger making off up the field, with my chicken in its mouth. I ran after it in my bare feet, shouting out and it stopped running after about fifty yards, dropping the bird, which half flew and half ran right out of sight, in the direction of the nearest woods. We both stood each other off and then the badger grunted and actually took a step towards me. I let him have the last word and went back to bed. I thought the fox would surely get that chicken, but no, she was back down in the yard the next morning – she never laid eggs in the wire again though.

Once I did get to Israel, I found I'd made a fair few friends at Kibbutz Ramot Menashe; most of them were volunteers from South America as it happened and I resolved to go out there and visit a few, as a premise for a Latin American adventure. I had been putting money aside for a while, with a plan to buy a Kawasaki Z900, but used that to buy US dollars for the six months away. Stuart from Kestrels was keen to get out and away from Kent too, so we bought plane tickets to Mexico City. We left in the first week of December and were supposed to make it to the Mardi Gras in Rio by February, but underestimated the size of the continent and the distances involved. We got into all sorts of scrapes on the way down and every day was an adventure. We'd made it south by land and water and joined the Amazon River, or Solimoes, as it's called at the three nations junction of Leticia, Tabatinga and Benjamin Constant, right on Carnival night. We didn't have the time or money to go any further south; not if we were going to get back to Mexico City by the deadline without cheating and taking a flight.

We did everything we could to make it an overland adventure, the highlight being the Darién Gap; ten days on foot from the last road in Panama to the first road in Colombia. It was January 1991 and the first Gulf War was ready to go. In the jungle there was no direct route, only tracks and trails linking primitive villages peopled by indigenous tribes, as well as the remains of African slave populations. It was a very lawless environment and many of the drunks from the black villages and the boatmen carried pistols as well as machetes. All the villages were sited on the banks of small meandering rivers, so some of the journey could be made by canoe, but didn't necessarily get us any further south. Once over the mountain pass at Palo de Las Letras we were into Colombia and the Atrato wetlands; totally impassable and I've never experienced mosquito swarms like what came down at Puente de Americas (Bridge of the Americas).

We met indigenous tribes, Colombian smugglers, armed Panamanian rangers and even came across an Irish missionary station; that's where I got bitten by a dog. The ironic thing was us in the middle of this inaccessible Central American jungle, meeting up with a couple of other adventurers who just happened to be an American (Bob from Pennsylvania) and an Israeli (Yaron from Tel Aviv). We had no communication with the outside world and the armies of each of our nations were probably fighting and dying in some featureless desert because of the 'black gold'. When we got through the other side, we learned that it was all over. A guest house owner in the banana port town of Turbo told us we were 'very great cowards', because we were not out there fighting with our people.

I got back from South America looking like a wild man. I'd lost a stone in weight, due to amoebic dysentery as well as the fact that I'd spent my last three weeks food budget on an open water diving course. My hair hadn't been touched for six months and I had a beard like a hedge.

Stuart went out and bought an old ambulance at auction and he kitted it out as a camper van. He lived in that and we saw less and less of him, as he was often working away. He'd given up butchery and become an engineer, working in the Gulf States, then New Zealand. He eventually settled in Tasmania.

The Duck, with its string of hopeless new owners, became our playground once again. Its days were numbered, with the high-speed rail link set to go right over top of the site. Each successive guardian put less and less effort into fostering a respectful clientele, so that towards the end, pretty much anything went, as long as people were still spending. Del's birthday party one Saturday night in January 92 featured a bit of a scuffle amongst us, with me slamming Matt Godden down against the Juke box, and then onto the Pool table, when he jumped on my back and tried to choke me out. I've known Matt since primary school and he never did know when to stop pushing. I found out the next day that he was in William Harvey with a ruptured kidney. I went in to see him and he was all stuck up with tubes in a hospital bed. He said he had noticed while he was still in the pub that he was pissing red, but he'd put it down to all the Pernod and Black he'd had.

Since that night it's become a bit of an unwritten rule that, every time we meet up at a do of some kind, there's going to be a bit of a ruck. I still usually win and did give him a black eye at his own 40th birthday bash.

# CHAPTER 7: THE WHITE CHARGER

I had been without a car since I'd sold the Friesian cow and it didn't bother me. But then, in May of 1992, I got the opportunity to buy Dad's C reg. Toyota Tercel, one of the early four wheel-drive estate cars on the market. Bright red it was, with good tyres and certainly the best car I'd had, or would have for quite some years to come. I kept the Tercel for two and a half years, which was a record for me. Also I kept it in reasonable condition, only having one slight accident during that time that, for once, wasn't even my fault. Coming down Harringe Lane back from Warehorne, I'd just rounded a bend and met a Datsun mini truck that locked up and jackknifed into me. He pulled it up broadside, blocking the road and just breaking one of my lights.

I went back to Scotland in the Tercel, primarily to climb Ben Nevis, before meeting up with a bloke called Terry to do some climbing on the Isle of Skye. He was over fifty, but walked me to exhaustion, as well as breaking my nerve crossing over the Cuillin Ridge. His actual job was a mountaineering expedition leader; I bumped into him some years later in the transit area at Bangkok airport: he was on his way to Burma.

Fast forward two years and I definitely had an international outlook on life. I'd not returned to the Americas, instead I'd gone east to Thailand, Burma, Indo-China and the Philippines. I'd got into Cambodia during the first few weeks of that communist country opening up to the world for independent travellers, and I immediately stumbled into the United Nations Transitional Authority. I had found a cause; world peace and humanitarianism and I knew I had to do something to help build the new world order.

By May 1994, the Bosnian war was probably at its most hopeless stage and that's when I answered an advert in the local paper calling for volunteers, with their own vehicles, to join an aid convoy to the former Yugoslavia. We were going to break the siege of Sarajevo and of course I was in! I roped Del Boy into the plan and the result was a wild wine-up night in my new caravan. We talked and planned and laughed the night away, drinking eight bottles of cheap wine between us. The last two bottles weren't necessary and the next morning I was chucking up along Beaver Road, whilst driving to Ashford Market to buy our supplies.

We needed a vehicle, and Dad donated us his old Ford Transit Crewbus; taxed, insured and MOT'd, in exchange for his BSA Super Rocket actually getting finished by the 28th of June. Dad had bought this crashed bike as a project years before; it was to be the super bike he had wanted as a teenager and this model was the A 10 version he had not been able to afford back in the 60s. I worked on that bike with every spare hour I had and it was virtually finished by the time we were set to leave. All gleaming chrome and sapphire blue paintwork together in one piece, just not quite ready to start.

So I'd inherited a C reg. MKII Transit, long wheelbase. It was a two litre petrol, with twin wheeled rear axel drive. By the time this old school bus was ready to load up, the 'White Charger', as she was christened, looked a sight to be proud of. We'd taken the bench seats out and caged off the cargo section with pig wire. I removed the bumper and bull bars from the old, by now deceased, 1600 tranny and bolted and welded them to the front of the 'Charger'. It had good tyres all round and two spares, which I secured to the custom roof rack Dad had made. Del and I rubbed and sanded down the old yellow paintwork, masked up and sprayed the whole thing UN white; to the sound of 'Under the Bridge' by the *Red Hot Chilli Peppers*. My taste in music had mellowed somewhat since the early days; the 80s was my Friday night and the 90s more like half way through the afternoon the day after, but a sunny day. I was listening to stuff like REM, Joan Osborne, Sting and even Tracy Chapman. Actually there was lots of good music around; it all reminds me now of either travelling in South East Asia or mechanicing back home at the barn. The CB radio aerial stuck on top of the roof was what made it all seem real, the 'Vehicle of Hope' was complete and we were ready to go.

We had the wheels, but needed petrol money and aid to take with it. Most of the aid we carried that time we had picked up from a collection point run by the organisers of the convoy. Some we collected ourselves, but gathering petrol money was much harder. Del and I did a boot fair stall at the Sellindge Steam Rally over the Whitsun bank holiday weekend; we were selling all kinds of junk and rusty crap. We had bought some cheap crates of dodgy soft drinks from the market to sell, as well as all the Cadburys Crème Eggs that Sellindge Stores had left over from Easter.

I now think about that passage in the book I saved from the fire, perhaps to represent the reality of the United Nations; growing rich and drunk on the business of world conflict and suffering. All the big organisations are corrupt, political or religious and where there is corruption there is abuse.

*Revelation Chapter 17 verses 1-2*

*Then one of the seven angels who had the seven bowls came and talked with me saying to me, 'Come, I will show you the judgement of the great harlot who sits on many waters, with whom the kings of the earth committed fornication, and the inhabitants of the earth were made drunk with the wine and her fornication.'*

*Revelation Chapter 18 verse 3*

*'For all the nations have drunk of the wine of the wrath of her fornication, the kings of the earth have committed fornication with her, and the merchants of the earth have become rich through the abundance of her luxury.'*

A Jehovah's Witness who had turned up at Kestrels years before had said to me 'All worldly governments are controlled by Satan', I thought the man was nuts. It's not the devil that's in control, it's the greed and desire of man. Humans are inherently corruptible, even the good ones. And there were some good ones on that convoy of hope.

We set off from Ramsgate port on 28th June in a snake-line of twenty two vehicles, mostly Transits, Renaults and Mercedes vans. Oostende was the landing point, most of us were first-timers so didn't know any of the other drivers and every vehicle had a co-driver. So that was forty four do-gooders all in all. I've got to be honest, we weren't all saints; there was the odd con-man, a few adventurers and a would-be mercenary.

Everyone new had hastily made up a CB 'handle', as their vehicle's call sign; if it didn't have a ring to it, we just forgot it and called people by some noticeable individuality. There was 'Brett Concrete', 'White Escort', 'Talbot Express', 'Seven and a Half Tonner' and 'Wheels of Steel' (I came up with that one), to name a few. I can't remember the lead vehicle's call sign but Duke and Mary were the 'back door'.

It was quite fun talking CB crap and working out who had a sense of humour and who we could wind up a bit.

It was baking hot from day one and the White Charger was an oven, it had no ceiling insulation. This was due to it having caught fire while Dad was welding on the roof rack anchors. The raw metal shell acted like a steel drum, with the noise from the road and the whirring of the propshaft reverberating within the space left above the food, clothing and medical aid we were carrying.

We stopped at the old East Germany border in the early hours and were off again by mid morning. All of us slept in our vans, but the others had left space for their own comfort; we had loaded every space we could. So Del got the front seats and I had to find space on top of the aid, just under the fire rusted roof panel.

We crossed into Austria near Passau, on the edge of the Alps and it was the first time I'd seen them. It was early evening by then and the tunnel under the mountains was so long, it was dark when we came out the other side. It did rain that night, the rain and the mountains reduced our radio capability to about half a mile and no one knew who was where. I set up a call system where each vehicle checked on the one in front and behind, this went up and down the line and finally the reports came back that all vehicles were accounted for. I felt a bit chuffed that it seemed to be me keeping the convoy together. We stopped for the night at the Gralla services and all went in for a meal and a beer; it turned into quite a few beers and we started to get to know each other.

Early next morning we were up and ready, crossing into Slovenia with its rolling hills and tall Mediterranean oaks, quaint little houses and 1930s type agriculture going on around us; people were still using horse drawn wagons, hand scythes and pitch forks. It was hard to believe that this beautiful little country had fought a brief war of independence with Serbia, only a couple of years previously. People waved and cheered us as we passed by and I knew we were doing something good.

The Adriatic coast was reached at the Croatian town of Crikvenica, where we stayed in a hotel car park. The night was so warm, we just slept out on the tarmac beside the vehicles – we didn't get much sleep. Del managed to engage the reversing alarm while I slept with my head beside the rear wheels. Then around 2 am, we were woken by Danny from the 'Purple Turtle' doing a good impression of an East European guard, torch light in our eyes and stern commands: we fell for it. About an hour later, some arsehole (no one owned up to it) squirted water in my face as I'd lain out asleep. I was quite angry actually.

In the morning we had a quick swim in the harbour and moved off. The intention was to reach Medjugorje inside the Bosnian Croat territories, but nothing went to plan.

The Adriatic Highway was a great driving road, like a long winding cliff edge. A lot of it was dry rocky coast with linear islands offshore, as well as some peninsulas where bridges had been destroyed and the road re-routed over temporary pontoons. The sea was deep blue and often quite a long drop down, with no real barriers to stop vehicles plunging off the edge. We did see several wrecked vehicles at the bottom of gorges and even in the sea.

It was warm outside, 31 degrees, but in our cab the temperature was 38, that's 105 Fahrenheit: we were driving a hot-house on wheels. Our radiator had started overflowing at Oostende and we could only keep the temperature stable during the slow bits as long as we had the heater on, with the fan blowing full force. This method took away as much heat as was possible from around the manifold, but it meant we were just wearing boxer shorts most of the time.

Vehicles started playing up: the Talbot had developed a fuel blockage problem back in Germany, and every now and then the driver would announce over the radio, 'The Talbot's losing power' or 'The Talbot is cutting out', it didn't like the uphill parts and we were always waiting for it. The Brett Concrete Transit got an air blockage and the Seven and a Half Tonner got a puncture; we couldn't believe he wasn't carrying a spare. Then there was the major calamity, which was an embarrassment to British engineering: the Land Rover Discovery had some kind of clutch failure. They transferred the trailer box it was pulling to someone else and towed him on a rope. The problem was he kept riding the brakes on the down hill gradients and burned them out into the bargain.

Jeff, otherwise known as 'Universal Soldier' wanted to make up a rigid tow-bar, but the team leaders weren't listening and quite a divide developed between the more practical new-comers and those old sweats running the show. We were parked up at a check-point, within range of the hills to the north; the Serbs had previously used those hills to shell the villages we had been driving through and it didn't feel comfortable. We were there for nearly three hours, while we waited for a mechanic who never arrived. Eventually, as the sun got low in the sky, the decision was made to carry on as we were into battle-scarred Zadar, a port town that had been heavily shelled, quite recently it looked. The evidence was clear to see: many buildings shot up and wrecked on the way in. We crossed a pontoon bridge that bypassed the original iron one; that now was broken, twisted and slumped into the sea, beside a half sunk ferry boat.

Finally we rumbled into the car park of the Calavary

Hotel; used by the UN peace keepers as well as it having become a temporary refugee shelter. The large car park was full of inquisitive children trying to scrounge stuff, as well as eight or nine UN vehicles. There were old women dressed in black and wearing head scarves, they were sitting around, knitting and embroidering.

We had a bit of a laugh with some of the Malaysian soldiers, who were out there, and Del swapped his waterproof for an UNPROFOR T-shirt, I can't remember what that stood for but someone got a pat on the back for making it up. A stroll on the beach brought the day to a close, the sun setting as a big red orb along the water line dissolved the problems the day had brought. After a communal meal washed down with some bar drinks, we took the party out into the car park. Quite late on, four or five six-wheeled British Army trucks turned up and their crews got out to a warm welcome. Most of us in the aid convoy were familiar enough with each other, by that time, to start becoming ratty about stuff. Brett and White Escort nearly had a scrap over the one female squaddie in the group; I don't think she was interested in either of them.

In the morning, reality set in and the planned ten o'clock meeting didn't happen, nor did the twelve o'clock. We lost a couple of vehicles; those drivers had decided to leave the convoy, because of all the disorganisation in general, but also people were starting to get a bit nervous about what might lie ahead. It was alright boasting about dodging snipers bullets and avoiding land mines, whilst joining in the CB banter on the road across Western Europe, quite another thing to be within a few hours of living it. It would have been more reassuring if we'd been getting regular updates, but we weren't and we didn't have a clue what was going on. Finally a rigid tow bar was made up out of a scaffolding tube and some chain, exactly what Jeff had suggested the day before.

So we didn't get on the road until about 2pm, and the plan was to tow the Discovery 120 kms down the coast, to the UN base at Split. Well that sounded uncomplicated and obviously the right thing to do. Most of us were just pleased to know that there was a plan, and that we were actually doing something.

Cock-ups were made all day long; we lost 'The Duke' (our rear guard vehicle), and some of us were worried in case it had gone over the edge. We'd already covered half the distance before one vehicle (without towing ability) was sent back to look out for them, half of us waited by the roadside whilst the Discovery and the others went on. The scout vehicle came back, but hadn't found a trace of them, so we had no choice but to get to Split before evening time. The Charger was now 'the back door' and when we rolled into Split and reunited with the convoy, we discovered that the Duke had got there before the lot of us; that old moustachioed fiend knew the country and had taken an inland route, without telling anyone! The other thing we found out was that we had lost another call sign; we'd missed the row, but were told that it was all about the way the mission was being managed and they'd gone their own way. We would lose another the following day. We did, however, pick up a couple of extra vehicles in Split. The drivers had been waiting for a convoy to tag along with into Bosnia. As far as we knew, no previous unsupported convoy of volunteers had made it into Sarajevo: we would be the first.

There was a mix of bravado, anxiety, determination and blind faith amongst us all as we set out from the UN base at 22:30 hrs, minus the Discovery. Driving into a war zone at night seemed unwise, but we were doing it. Del and I wore our flack jackets for the first time, NATO helmets were ready to grab should we come under fire. The road wound up and up into the mountains and it was so hot, even at night. I, for one, was dead tired and came close to messing up once, when I almost didn't pull out of a bend in time. After that, I got Del to splash water in my face and down my neck periodically, to keep me alert.

The convoy took a wrong turn down a restricted road, the mistake was realised once we were all fully committed and it turned into quite a situation. The lead vehicles turned around, but the ones behind me with trailers couldn't. So we sat there for a moment with the hazards on; then White Charger and Wheels of Steel took command of the situation. Del and Jeff guided the coupled vehicles back up the slope for about two hundred yards; it was quite a steep curving road with a drop on our left. When the Army Forward Command arrived up the hill in front of me (they were using hand sprayed VW vans), four soldiers got out, very suspicious, sharp and edgy. I was the one who got confronted by a commander who looked like Ratko Mladić. They were Croats, not Serbs; but at 03:30hrs, within shooting range of the border, they were anything but friendly.

Well, we got ourselves out of that, and to the designated crossing point about half an hour later, allowing ourselves three hours' sleep: we were supposed to move out at 7am. By 9am we had been turned away, the reasons weren't communicated back down the line: we were just re-routed to the only other option, a picturesque little town on the Neretva River called Metković. We waited there for three hours; it was 100 Fahrenheit outside in the shade and well over that in our steel drum.

We didn't get through that one either: I heard it was

a matter of graft payments per vehicle, probably was, although the fact we wanted to aid the Muslims in Mostar and Sarajevo wouldn't have impressed the Bosnian Croats. They were fighting the same enemy, but they weren't allies. I didn't know it then, but humanitarian aid is politics and business – anyone who says it's all for love is as deluded and naïve as we were then, or just lying.

As would be expected, we were all pretty low on the drive back to Split. Three call signs remained there with the crippled Discovery: 'Robin's Nest', 'El Corazon' and the 'Duke-Mobile'. I was sorry to lose Duke and Mary, they were genuine people; pensioners who'd bought a motor home and made aid trips part of their lifestyle. It wasn't the last we'd see of them though, our paths would cross again.

We had a new guide and leader in 'Uncle George' and his Essex outfit, Humanitarna Pomoć. George was driven by faith, as a reformed casino gambling addict. El Corazon (who'd got us all out there) on the other hand, was a reformed alcoholic. Apparently he'd seen the light while at his low point on Deal beach one night. We'd been joking about that story, suggesting it was probably a paramedic's torch beam.

First we had to get back to Zadar, and the drive started off in the afternoon heat with us rolling down a long straight run, a bank falling away to our right and a steep drop to the sea on our left. Del needed freshening up to stay awake at the wheel, so I tried to flick water from a flimsy polythene bag into his face. I misjudged it and whipped him across both eyes. Probably one of the stupidest things I've ever done – there was the lighter incident too, that I sparked up under his armpit to stop him holding the wheel incorrectly; he would keep leaning forward and steering like a speedway rider. Of course it was baking hot and that Links aerosol deodorant that we'd brought, left over from our Steam Rally stall, was still flammable, no matter how much you sweated. So Del screamed with the shock, like Homer Simpson, with both hands over his eyes. I had to grab the wheel and hold it steady, whilst screaming a bit myself to start with – it was surreal. 'Don't do anything! Take your feet off the pedals! I've got the wheel! I've got the wheel!!' He still doesn't know why he reacted like that; perhaps I flicked him out of a nightmare. Well, we got the bus under control and I steered her into the bend at the bottom of the straight, as Del started to sort himself out. Five minutes later we were laughing about it and cracking jokes over the CB.

Everyone was so tired, and tempers were just below the surface for a lot of us, with several people flipping out verbally over the next day or so. George was a calming influence though, he kept us talking and that kept us awake.

The next day found us waiting around at Zadar until one thirty in the afternoon. We had all had a swim at least, and there was no great panic by now. We were all still fully loaded, but we had been all week, so another day didn't really matter. Then George gave the words we all wanted to hear: we were moving out. We'd had no contact with the others back at Split, so the Discovery was not going to be joining back up. I know they all did get home eventually, but twenty-odd vehicles couldn't just sit around with no updates; people had jobs to get back to, rental agreements on the vans to honour, and most of us didn't have an inexhaustible supply of cash. It was all Deutschemarks and Kuna (Del ran out of both) – everything is so easy nowadays with smart technology and ATM machines. People don't have to be responsible in the way we were used to being, back when no one I knew had a mobile phone or a computer, and everyone who wanted to get somewhere had to carry enough cash for emergencies, and know how to read a map. Life is so devoid of genuine circumstances now; most people don't seem to even own a wrist watch, let alone a compass.

We were heading up to a small Croatian town on the front line called Gospić, and to start with we had a twenty-kilometre hill to climb. The White Charger, with only four gears, motored ahead and gave out sit-reps. Away from the coast, it was a much harder and more isolated world; I didn't think it would have looked much different to how it must have been in the 1940s.

We rolled into the town behind a police escort, Union Jacks fluttering from aerials and roof racks and we were saluted by soldiers at the check-points along the way. There was no doubt that we were a popular attraction that day. People cheered or just stared from their windows; cars flashed their lights and sounded horns. We felt pretty good. Once inside the town, the atmosphere was more muted and it didn't look as if many buildings had escaped the recent fighting unmarked. There were bullet holes and shrapnel scars spattering the walls, shell holes in the roads and pavements, and the spire was missing from the top of the church.

The town police extended their hospitality and we were given food and drink at the station. The building had been fortified with sand bags and tree trunks, stacked at a sloping angle against the walls all round, to deflect and absorb the incoming metal. The building itself showed plenty of evidence of a desperate fire fight; with bullet holes in the door, fired from the inside out. We unloaded some of the gear at the Red Cross centre, another load went off to a warehouse attached to the hospital and a third we dropped at a bullet-riddled school building at the neighbouring village of Perušić.

I got an early night, half past midnight, while some of the others got drinking the local fire water (Slivovitz) with the gun-toting paramilitary escorts, until I don't know what time. In the early morning sunlight, Del turned up drunk and started to get into the driver's door of the Charger. That was a short argument. I drove us across the hills and down to join the coast again at Senj, it all started to feel a bit like a holiday then, there was a lot of clear land between us and any of the fighting.

We lost another couple of call signs, one being Terry Sullivan (the same Terry I teamed up with in Scotland a month or so later): their vans were now empty and they wanted to make their own way home. We were then down to about twelve or thirteen vehicles by the time we reached Rijeka, the most northerly of the large towns on the Croatian Adriatic coast.

The Talbot broke down again. It wouldn't draw fuel, so we set up a supply from a jerry can in the cab; we used plastic tubing from a box of catheters someone was carrying as medical aid. It was all held together with insulating tape and cable ties, but it worked.

By late afternoon we had reached a refugee camp called Hidroelektra, near the entrance to the Učka tunnel. We all stacked the majority of our goods into seven piles, each one to be divided up among the occupants of the seven single story buildings. They looked a bit like long scout huts, themselves divided into about eight small rooms, one for each family living there. I handed out Derek's sleeping bag along with our aid – for a laugh, and because I was sick of the sight of it. He knew what I'd done, but let it go all the same.

The rain came down at last and that was our signal to go; we drove through the night to our last stop, a well organised refugee camp on a school premises just across the Slovenian border. We camped out there and divided out what we had left, which was mostly sweets and toys, to the kids there in the morning. There was nothing more to do before the long drive home, twenty four hours, virtually non-stop motoring. I took the back door and Universal Soldier was the lead vehicle, although he wasn't even in his original Mercedes Sprinter. Jeff had jumped vehicles to ride along with a slightly odd pigeon-toed redhead, towing the 'Period Interiors' trailer box behind her Vauxhall Frontera. There were no real dramas on the drive back, the atmosphere had lightened since Gospić and we were all getting along fine. We were tired but comfortable when we drove off the ferry ramp at Ramsgate; the White Charger had clocked up three thousand miles and not missed a beat. For me, it was the best thing I'd ever done. I had arrived.

# CHAPTER 8: HIDROELEKTRA

There were two more convoys the White Charger managed that year. One in September with Uncle George and one with Tony and 'Convoj Nade' again, just before Christmas. They were extra milestones to clock up, but neither could match that first dash for martyrdom: not in the size or pure exuberance of it all. We'd driven like a bunch of cowboys on that original trip; pulling stunts for fun, we'd come up alongside other drivers, undertaking on the hard shoulder to exchange snacks and drinks etc. Then there was the tailgating game I'd played, driving up so close behind the vehicle in front of me so that I could try and work out what tyres they were running on by the look of the spare. This started because I was trying to prove a point that we could all bunch up tighter, to make sure that the line didn't get dissected by regular vehicles cutting in and splitting us up: this was happening often and it really mattered.

I never could understand the point of road-rage, I treated the road like a free for all – the whole point of it was that you were moving along, not getting bogged down in some blinkered vendetta because someone else had a loss of attention moment. The worst incident I've ever experienced was on the autobahn that September; I suppose I'd cut in front of a Polish artic driver a bit close on the overtake and he sounded his horns and flashed his lights: all right, that was me told. Five minutes later he came roaring through, running me onto the hard shoulder. I took it in my stride as I was on the ball; dropped back to come around him and into the middle lane, but the bastard was brandishing a club hammer out of the window at us. I actually believe he wanted to kill us, he was weaving between the two lanes to stop me getting ahead and out of harm's way and I felt very vulnerable: the autobahn isn't the M20 with a speed limit and an escape slip-road every few miles. We got by and caught up with the group; there wasn't anything else to do. I did think we might have an encounter at the next fuel stop if he was tailing us, and we kept a look out, images of that 1971 film *Duel* with Dennis Weaver came to mind.

In preparation for the December run, back to Gospić and Hidroelektra, I had managed to collect all my own aid. I even had the roof rack stacked with old bicycles (seventeen of them), so the young people at the isolated camp could get out to find work, etc. Guy from the Oakmen motorcycle club had helped me to organise a raffle at the Woolpack pub in Brabourne; it brought in a hundred and one pounds to help with petrol. Donations came in from elsewhere too; the village of Tilmanstone held a fund raiser in the village hall and I got a new co-driver out of it. Julian just happened to be one of my older sister's public school friends; Lyn had gone to the Girls' Grammar and had a more elevated class of pals than I did, plus she was cleverer than me so, unlike myself, she chose her friends from a pool of potential high achievers. I'm not saying my friends were all thick, although undoubtedly there were some of a less advanced intellectual bent, who were fine with that and knew their limitations.

Julian was a bit unusual to start with, we stayed at a hotel on the coast one night, and he had to go out to the van to get his personal pillow, saying he could only lay his head on duck down. I like to learn, and I did borrow a few tips from him. I also nearly killed us both, after Gospić on that long road down the mountain to Senj. It was a rainy night and we were the forth convoy vehicle to overtake an artic, on one of the few straight sections of that road. Car headlights were coming up the hill faster than I'd anticipated and I was fully committed. I had to keep my foot on the floor and was able to nip in front of the lorry (Julian said it locked up) with no more than feet to spare either side of us. That was more than reckless: it was damn stupid and so lucky that we all made it. I did apologise to Julian, after I finished shrieking in triumph. I apologised a couple of years later too, when I met him down at the Sellindge Steam Rally. If I ever see him again, I'm going to apologise once more.

I was getting careless with the van, it's true, and there were a couple of minor crashes during the last days of December. I broke a rear light (reversing again) and then there was a momentary loss of control on the lane near me, where I slid around a bend and got snagged up against the fence. No real damage done and then the year was over. I wouldn't drive a car again for six months.

# CHAPTER 9: TRANS-SIBERIAN EXPRESS

I was twenty eight years old when, just after Christmas 1994, I left England, very alone, on a jetfoil from Ramsgate to Oostende. I had said goodbye to friends and family, some of whom I would never see again. I was going off to see the world, take part in it and absorb it. I wanted to cast my life into the wind and see what came back. I wasn't content to live a regular boring life, making sensible decisions, holding down a job so's I could go down the pub of an evening for a game of pool, then back home to watch some crap on the TV. I couldn't see me settling down with a local woman either, I don't even think I fancied them anymore. British women were so opinionated, but worst of all, most of the ones I knew just acted like blokes anyway. I liked Latin women, Orientals too, and anything tribal I found fascinating. Everything had to be exotic, exciting and with a touch of danger thrown in. However that may sound, meeting foreign women was not my reason for travelling. I simply needed to experience the world and taste it, live it.

It was all planned out: to China by train, all five thousand plus miles of it, starting from Oostende. I had a Lonely Planet guide book for China and I would get myself to Hong Kong, then decide what came next. As well as my heavy rucksack full of clothes and essentials, I had a day pack and two holdalls; the largest one was full of books: everything I thought I might like to read during the year and a day I planned to be away. I would read them, then sell them on or swap them with other travellers for guide books to the countries ahead. I didn't actually take much money, my plans included working as and where I could, or needed to. Whatever was going to be would be.

The first train only took me to Brussels, where I changed to a sleeper, bound for Moscow. From Moscow, a Russian train took me to Siberia and from Irkutsk a Chinese train completed the journey through Mongolia to Beijing. The best way of explaining how it was to travel right across the communist continent in 1995 is to rely on the pages of my journal written at the time. I will quote sections from that journal; this is how I recorded the experience:

**Wednesday, December 28<sup>th</sup> 1994**
"The Jetfoil took off like a plane, quite exciting, over a pretty rough grey sea. I felt the anticipation rise in me, to discover new lands and rediscover old ones.

At Oostende, I felt the strain of carrying 90lb (about 35kilos of luggage in my assortment of bags. Belgium looked flat, dull, overcast and very wet, a lot of ground water. I finished the tea my mum had made me, in the tiny little brown thermos flask that I used to take to school with my packed lunch at age eleven. At Brussels I changed trains and boarded the European express to take me to Moscow. The corridor was very narrow and I could not find my sleeping compartment, nor could I turn around in the corridor. So I had a ridiculous shuffle up and down, twice, to find it. It was the size of a toilet, but my Belarusian room mate seems fine. I'm glad there are just the two of us, though it apparently seats three.

It was very hot on the top bunk, 85°f, and stuffy. There was no room to stretch out or sit up, and during the night another Russian man joined our compartment on the middle bunk.

### 29th December, Thursday
I didn't get up until 10:20 East European time, with three to a compartment they are like cupboards.

We spent most of the day rumbling through Poland. It looks sort of rustic, all farm houses with small fields, very flat and muddy, no snow yet. It was corrugated iron roofs and wood stacks, the outskirts of Warsaw were surrounded with quaint Gypsy style sort of allotment huts with smoking chimneys. Also many homes made of old railway carriages. I did not see anything of Warsaw city, as the train line goes underground to the central station. This is a very depressing, dark, poorly lit, wet, bare place of black concrete. The Polish customs police, acting in typical surly form, stamped my passport upside down and on top of my Mongolian visa. We crossed the partially frozen River Bug, which is the border between Poland and Belarus and also where the Nazis invaded the Soviet Union from, during the Second World War. At Brest, the first town in Belarus, the train stopped in a sort of hanger to change the axels. The railways in the Soviet Union are a wider gauge than Europe. It was a dark, cold, depressing place to work. Some of the men out there in filthy tattered clothes looked so miserable.

At 11pm, the train stopped at Minsk and most of the passengers got off. Egor left, so I could sleep on the bottom bunk and avoid the rising cigarette smoke.

### Friday, December 30th 1994
Well I can see snow, pine trees, silver birch. We are in Russia. It does not look very cold outside. The houses are funny little

two or three story pine built things, with twin pitched roofs. On the outskirts of the towns there are many allotment style huts with fenced off gardens; maybe they are allotments, but they have chimney pots too. I saw a snowball fight for the first time in years, also many Russians walking around in big coats with fur collars and those bearskin hats. The Soviet transport insignia is on trucks and trains and I begin to see all the trucks which were so common in Vietnam.

Well, the train arrived earlier than I had thought it would and I am now here in Moscow in the Hotel Belgrad. My Intourist escort, who did not have a car, met me at the Belarusian train station. He was holding a limp piece of paper with TALLER written on it. A bit of bureaucracy at the hotel reception and then I went for a stroll. After half an hour I reached the Kremlin: it looks magnificent. I did not go inside as it was late, but I walked around. I couldn't believe it when I saw a man in a kilt and an old green Barbour jacket and green Hunter wellies. I had to speak with him and, yes, he was from Scotland. He too was disappointed with the warmer than average weather. Red Square was not disappointing, despite St. Basil's Cathedral being smaller than it looks. I walked around the walls and over the Moskva River bridges. I tried to get back to my hotel on the underground, but it was hopeless, still it certainly was worth seeing. Built in the 1930s, the metro stations were all chiselled marble, with C19th style fittings of wood and brass: a remarkable public utility.

### Saturday, December 31st
New Year's Eve

I had more luck today with the Metro and managed to get to Alexandetsky Sud station, near the Kremlin. It seems my fake student card that I bought in Bangkok has paid off;

they let me into the Kremlin for half price. The cars parked outside the Presidium of the Supreme Soviet were not very posh, some were black Mercedes with tinted windows, but most were just old Ladas and the giant statue of Lenin was gone, only the base and some railings remained.

I forced myself to stay up till 10:30 to go to the New Year's Eve celebration in Red Square, Arbat Street was dead, and in fact the whole city was closed down. I was surprised, and hungry. It was drizzling and the streets were slippery. I walked along Alexander Garden, under the Kremlin walls and, as I passed the Tomb of the Unknown Soldier, a policeman in a black greatcoat, jackboots and Russian hat kicked a local man in the stomach, for what reason I couldn't see. I got a truer picture of Moscow tonight: not just rich Muscovite families wrapped up in fur, doing their late Christmas shopping, but the working classes, the people, the proletariat. It was them who came out to see the New Year in.

As I entered Red Square, it was only ten percent full, the weather was miserable and nothing much was happening. A television camera appeared and gradually some more people. I had thought that the state would put on a fireworks display but no, so I went in search of a refreshment stall. I found the only one still open, just around the corner, and it took ages to get served. At 11:50, hordes of people started pouring out of the Metro station, all in high spirits, and I joined them walking back to the square. The rain had turned to light sleet and as soon as I got there it snowed, big flakes, just before midnight and for five minutes after. The square was full of people, drinking cheering and letting off fireworks – it was quite a scene. Some people were very drunk, some were angry, but most were happy: not the police though. I saw a Canadian flag and a New Zealand one, a Lebanon flag and a Union Jack; they were all together in an international group. A girl said 'Nova Buena' to me, so I didn't feel left out anymore. By Lenin's Tomb, there was a group of die-hard Soviets with a megaphone, all singing and dancing under the hammer and sickle.

### 1st January 1995, Sunday
I was up late; I took my breakfast in the hotel restaurant, even worse than yesterday's. I went to the local bakery and queued up to buy bread and cheap British lemonade. I had to buy a tin of Danish corned beef from the hotel shop, as there was no other food for sale. By the time I got back to my room it was just gone 12:00 and I found that my door card had switched off at 12:00: very smart.

Intourist drove me to the Yaroslavskaya railway station to catch my four day train to Irkutsk. This station serves the East and it was full of a much poorer class of people than the one that leads to the West. I have a bottom bunk, in a much more spacious four berth compartment. Only me and a young business type Russian, who was still drunk from the night before. The conductor (provodnik) and his girlfriend ripped me off for three dollars for bed sheets. They wanted another ten for my extra baggage too, but I wasn't having that.

The snow has laid outside the city and there are a lot of pine trees, silver birch also. When I boarded the train, the Scorpions and Nirvana were playing through the speakers, nothing of interest since.

### 2nd January, Monday
The land has become slightly undulating, towns and villages are few and far between, and we are back to small pine wood houses with pitched corrugated iron roofs. I noticed at one

stop, that even in the cold snow and ice, someone was still selling ice creams.

Alexei (my room mate) shared his breakfast with me: bread, a sort of relish made from tomatoes, onions, carrots and aubergines, and the main delicacy, raw salted thick pork blubber. We had Vietnamese tea, and then Alexei bought a bottle of vodka. The way to drink it is in large amounts and down in one. We shared this bottle, approximately one pint, and talked and laughed about military politics, among other things. The Russian army had entered Grozny in the Chechen conflict.

I was reasonably drunk, but foolishly agreed to another bottle. Disaster followed; I had to excuse myself, then I fell asleep. In the night I was out and throwing up again and I got no sleep after 3am. It's so hot in the compartment, 30 °C, I can hardly stand it.

## January 3rd, Tuesday

The sunrise was nice against the snow, dotted with green trees, but I couldn't appreciate it. I remember the last time I drank vodka, when I was seventeen, and the same thing had happened. It took me a couple of hours to rouse myself, dress and get out of the room, I really wanted to rinse my mouth out, but just before I got to the toilet the door was locked, as we were coming into Omsk. The station looked very interesting; I would very much have liked to have got out and had a walk around in the cold, buy some fruit for later and take some pictures, but I felt sick again and didn't dare leave my place at the toilet door. It was packed snow on the platform and little red Zetor tractors with snow chains pulled luggage trailers around. It was bright sunshine, and people were walking around in fur coats, hats and boots, some pulling little sledges with their goods and belongings on.

I was relieved when the train moved again and the toilet door was opened – I hadn't thought I was going to last and, sure enough, I was retching until there was nothing left except the foul taste of vodka. I discovered from other passengers that we had passed through the Ural Mountains yesterday afternoon. I'd missed it while Alex and I had been drinking. Now everything is very flat, with wide expanses of snow, pine and birch trees. There are industrial towns from time to time and some little villages with little peasant cottages; these places have a communal well, I saw a man returning from one with a milk churn on a sledge.

I got out at the next stop, there was an old woman begging and she was crying, her face was blue. I gave her my last hundred ruble note, then my coins, and I felt so guilty I gave her the rest of the remaining six dollars I had in my wallet. She kept thanking me, but didn't really know how much it was. Alex changed it for her and gave me back my six dollars. My New Year's resolution is: to put back into the world evenly, as I accept its goodwill. And it's working already.

One thing I have noticed is that both my compasses have reversed and are telling me that I'm travelling west. This cannot be, so I assume it must be the effect of the overhead cables from which the train picks up its power. The temperature inside my carriage is ridiculous; it is now 91ºF – 33ºC. Outside now (at the last stop, Novosibirsk) the platform notice panel showed – 5º , 16:40 and a radiation count of P – 750; this is approximately three times higher than the average in Europe.

There is a miserable looking woman with a child moved into my compartment; she seems to have taken over Alexei's bed, the kid has three horrible friends who are now intruding on my peace of mind with plastic guns and transformers. The provodnik, who makes me think of a simple but amusing woodland creature, crossed with a mischievous troll and Timothy Spall, suggests that I move into Daphne's compartment. Daphne is a New Zealander with a hand missing; she has a good supply of English tea.

### Wednesday, 4th January
I wake at the break of dawn and there is an orange band, low on the horizon, which never really goes away. I don't know how far north we are, but the sun doesn't rise far. The Taiga is the name for the Siberian forest, fir trees and silver birch, I saw little else all day. My watch is still Moscow Time, which is five hours behind, so the sun sets at 11:00 – 12:30 by my watch. The scenery is more interesting now: rolling open country, trees and not too far between settlements. The sky is an almost unbelievable orange, lending an orangey-pink tinge to the snow on the ground and on the trees. I talked to Alexei about the compasses indicating west, he said the heaters are powered by 6000 volts.

This evening I could sleep only three hours out of the twelve left on this train. I'd not been bored at all on this journey, only uncomfortable and I just wanted to get out and walk.

### Thursday, 5th January
At last we arrived at Irkutsk main station. It was cold, the information reader showed - 6°. There was no transfer waiting for me, so Alex decided that I should go with him by taxi to his brother's house in the suburbs. The ride was fun in the packed snow, the driver never lost traction and it was still dark. Alex's brother's house is not extravagant,

just an apartment in a typical Soviet block. It's cold in the stairwell, the burned and crumbling concrete service steps belong in a multi story car park and the tiny apartment is dirty, stuffy and run down; not what I'd expected for a well off business family. The way they lived and how they looked in their home was like a low class council estate family; with dirty washing and dodgy wiring, shapeless polyester clothing that no one could feel good in. Hours later, when we all walked out, they had transformed into a fine looking middle class pair in nice city clothes.

Well, Alex made me eat cake and cold jellied chicken, and we drank a lot of tea. I said I needed to get to my hotel to have a shower, but they insisted that I should use their bathroom. I wished I had not done so, as from the hot tap came the coldest water I have ever showered in, it was enough to make my fingers numb within the minute I was under it. I went through it, as I didn't want them to think Englishmen couldn't hack Siberia, it hurt my scalp! Alex went in next and came out without comment, I asked him how it was and he said he forgot to tell me that the blue and red coloured tap tops are on the wrong taps. Just after first light we left in their car, the pink foggy dawn tinted everything. Irkutsk is so different to anywhere I have been before. These people are excellent cold weather drivers; they have no snow chains, only good chunky tyres on their Ladas. We arrived at the large Intourist hotel, where the reception was very frosty. Apart from Alexei, it seems that Russian people don't have much of a sense of humour. My printout says full board and they don't believe that it means three meals, so they had to phone Moscow. Then they begrudgingly gave me the meal vouchers and the staff in the hotel restaurant were even more begrudging. I went out for a three hour walk and the cold seized up my lips and made my eye lids feel strange. The town seemed quite picturesque, like a Christmas card. The snow on the verge, the hedges and the trees is a very fine powdery dry snow, it looks almost like frosted layers of fog. There is no wind and the air is clean. The people are walking around all muffled up, some pulling small sledges. I found the river and people were out on it ice fishing.

### Friday, 6th January

I had a rushed breakfast, as I was expecting Alex to come for me; I waited until 11:30 and he did not arrive. I got called to the service bureau and told that Moscow had not authorised full board for me and they confiscated my meal card. I walked to the bus station and nearly got squashed between a bus and a tram. I had wanted to go to Listuyanka, on the Baikal, but the bus had left at 09:30. I wasn't too upset, as it was supposed to take two and a half hours. I walked back down Karl Marx Street and there were vendors selling food, furs and ice creams. Ridiculous as it was, I bought an ice cream which gave me an instant headache. Alex did ring the hotel at 10:30 that evening, actually Russian Orthodox Christmas Eve. I have celebrated Christmas Eve thrice this year: December the third in Croatia, the twenty fourth in England and now the sixth of January in Russia. That's pretty good going.

Nothing was going on at the hotel, so we walked around the town, searching vainly for a restaurant open late. I nearly froze, but we had no luck so went back to the hotel and drank cherry tea in my room until one forty five am.

### Saturday, 7th January 1995

The Intourist taxi took me to the train station for 8am

and it was still dark. I bought a hot dog, which was surprisingly good.

I am on a Chinese train now. The staff are more friendly and respectful, the top windows open and the heating is moderate, but the toilets stink. For two hours or more we ran along the shore of Lake Baikal, the deepest lake in the world. It was frozen over at some of the shallower parts near the shore and I saw a jeep wheel-spinning on the ice at a small tributary. There are quite a lot of westerners on this train and Daphne is in the next carriage. The Russian customs at Dozine made a long evening of it; removing panels etc. searching for contraband. The Chinese passengers had lots of it, including two cockatoos and a Pekingese dog! The cockatoos had been sewn into pillows, but I do not know how they hid the dog.

### Sunday, 8ᵗʰ January

Ulan Bator has to be the coldest capital city in the world. It was just after sunrise and I left the train to take a walk around the block. I felt my nose hairs freeze with every breath I took in and only got to the road behind the station; I had to hurry on round as my fingers hurt so bad. The Mongols looked fierce and extremely hardy, many were dressed in their traditional thick felt tunics and funny shaped hats. It's not a big city and no tall buildings, high hills with a thin coating of pink snow can be seen not too far away. It's harsh here.

The train moved through the countryside and the hills flattened out to become an endless plain, sparsely inhabited, just small groups of yurts (Mongolian tents) surrounded by palisade fences, herds of cattle, goats and horses. There was the occasional small brick or concrete town. One town we stopped at called Choyr was memorable; it was a nowhere place, everything was covered in black coke dust, even the snow didn't lay. There were some mechanics on the platform and two small boys were hanging around; they asked me for food. They had those funny round faces with slitty eyes and hats with ear flaps. I gave them one third of a Toblerone bar each, they didn't know what it was, but when they started to eat it they were happy and they gave me a small Mongolian coin. One English bloke was out on the platform taking photos and the train started to pull out, no whistle, nothing; he was lucky to get back in.

The plain is vast and it's so cold, I saw deer and buzzards, we just passed a horseman with a herd of Bactrian camels. The snow on the ground is light and powdery with scrub grass showing through. The bare earth can be seen now, it's well below freezing but there is no moisture to bind it together. Actually I believe this is the Gobi Desert, flat vast, with no boundaries. The sun went down about four thirty and I got some sleep.

At the Chinese border they searched the compartment again, and we had to get out while the bogies were changed back to Chinese/European gauge. The border town we spent two and a half hours at was called Erenhot or Erlian. We changed some money and all went off to eat at a tiny Chinese/Mongolian restaurant. It was late in the evening and the place was heated with a single pot stove in the centre of the room. It only had four tables and we took up two of them, there were many stools though and the other customers looked to be railway employees and customs. It was the best Chinese meal I have ever eaten, hot and spicy. We all had small bowls and chopsticks and the dishes just kept coming, placed in the centre for everyone to help themselves. There was Mongolian tea, they said it had milk in it but it only had a faint cloudy complexion, it tasted strange. The meal was on Huan Ping, a young Chinese student who had just made a packet on smuggling his black market goods from Moscow to China. We drank beer and ate our fill, then walked back to the train around two thirty in the morning; it was bitterly cold and a light wind blew around the platform, everyone had thick hats on with ear and neck flaps.

We were all in high spirits boarding the train, the conductors too, as I suppose they were making money as well. The Chinese wanted to continue celebrating and chose my compartment, so we all crowded in, drank more beer and sang songs until 4am.

## Monday, 9th January

I woke up from a series of short dreams with a dry mouth and throat; the sun had just risen over the mountains between Jining and Datong. This was still Inner Mongolia, just before the Wall. The snow has all but disappeared and the steep, rugged mountains are a light brown earthy colour. Coming down into Datong, there were lots of interesting sights; people driving horse carts, traction carts and trucks with trailers full of coal. There are small terraced mud brick houses with round Chinese arches with those classic roof tiles, it was all single pitched roofs. We passed a steam engine, chugging away on the siding with clouds of smoke and steam, and there were other old diesel engines in use; every activity seems to be geared around production and transportation of coal. The coal burning power station we passed was so incredible, I forgot to take pictures. The pollution it kicked out was unbelievable: belching great clouds of dirty brown smoke from every orifice. It blotted out the sun and turned the clear blue sky into a heavy smog, completely covering Datong city – everything for miles around was covered in soot. Just after the train left the station, we passed through a short tunnel. I was looking out of the window and noticed four or five men crossing the lines, there was lots of shouting from the rear carriage, as bundles and bags were being thrown out. Then two or three Chinese jumped out of the back of the train; this was a contraband drop off and the buyers must have boarded the train at Datong station. I don't know how the Russians failed to find most of the stuff, but what was funny was the cooperation of all the passengers and train staff, everyone was in on it.

I caught my first sight of the Great Wall soon after: a long section running along the bottom of a mountain line, then it snaked up and over it. There were constant sightings for most of the rest of the journey; it was really like a wide tall pale causeway with towers about every mile. It went over hills and mountains, plains and river banks. We passed between ruined sections of the wall two or three times, as well as across a giant frozen, flooded valley bed, a shallow lake it looked like, with bits of wall running across it. At Qinglongqiao we passed through a tunnel and stopped at the station, it was built between the wall sections in the pass where there would have been a gate originally. The mountains rose up on either side and the wall clung to the ridges, so steep.

We arrived in Beijing about 5pm and I went with Takesh, a Japanese traveller, to the Qiaoyuan Hotel, three US dollars for a dorm room. It was cold inside and the girl on reception was clearly wearing several layers of summer clothes (apart from the hats and great coats they wear, the Chinese don't seem to have winter clothing, it's just clothing). She was sobbing, without any facial expression, as she checked us in, and our Taiwanese room mate Norman said 'That's

incredible! How can she check people in when she is crying?'
The poor girl became normal again without any sort of
transitional phase, then she sold us tickets to see acrobats
and opera. Norman got us fake Chinese student cards from
a kiosk next to the hotel, these get you ¾ discounts on a lot
of ticket prices and you get to pay in local currency (Yuan),
rather than FEC (Foreign Exchange Certificate). It is still
freezing outside, cold enough to give me a headache. We
went to get Peking duck to take back to the room.

### Thursday, 12th January
Norman and I wanted to go to Badaling (70 kms away)
to visit the restored part of the wall – we had to take four
different busses to get there and it was so cold. It was low
season and all the Chinese (including Norman) stopped at
the first tower going up the hill, so I had the place to myself
after that. We were able to get a single route bus back, but
it ran out of diesel just outside Beijing, so we had to finish
the journey by taxi.

### Friday, 13th January
I went to the Museum of Natural History. Most of the
museum was quite interesting: prehistory, insects, etc. There
were badly stuffed animals and unpleasantly displayed
snakes and marine life in jars. And then, in the final room,
the most disgusting display of exhibits imaginable. It was
all humans and all sorts of human body parts, dissected and
put in glass jars. There were three whole bodies: two men,
skinned, except for the ears, genitals and finger tips, they
were standing up. The dead woman was naked, except for
her black socks and a black sheet draped over her head. Her
chest and abdomen were opened up. There were dissected
genitalia, heads and deformed babies on display. The genitals

of an adult hermaphrodite were interesting I suppose, but I doubt the owner had volunteered to make that donation.

After that cultural experience, I visited the Temple of Heaven at Tiantan Park. Old men were flying kites, children were playing, couples were having their photographs taken and all the while discretely placed speakers wafted out classical Chinese music.

### Saturday, 14th January
I left Beijing today. There must have been three to four thousand people inside the railway station building, more outside. In the toilets, most of the doors were missing from the cubicles offering no privacy to those squatting over the holes, froth was welling up from the central drain and the large circular hand washing trough had the bog brushes standing up in it.

### Sunday 15th January
I arrived in Xian, capital of Shaanxi Province at about 6am. Xian is central China, so I've left the freezing temperatures behind, but it's still winter and smoggy here, due to a lot of coal fired industry. I caught a bus 30 kms out to see the terracotta warriors; this is the third bus I've been on with engine trouble. Chinese New Year is approaching and train tickets are rapidly becoming gold dust.

### Monday, 16th January
I did the city tour today, visiting the sites and riding on busses, bought a little red book of Mao quotations for 20 Yuan, about 2,1/2 dollars. Getting a bus back to the dorm hotel was difficult; they were all full to busting. I joined about twenty people who forced and squeezed themselves through the door, into the coughing, spitting mass. They

all have bronchitis and will cough in your face as you stand there. The minibus from the hostel to the train station broke down; the conductor poured an enamel bowl full of water into the steaming engine compartment. The engine cover was actually inside the bus, which caused it to fill with fumes.

## Tuesday, 17th January

This train carriage is dirtier that the one from Beijing, but the one family above, below and opposite my seat are friendly. The countryside is no longer frozen and actually has some real greenery; it's mainly flat with the odd hill. I'm heading east and my watch strap keeps breaking. Towards the end of the journey, I could see mud brick houses with thatched roofs, and not just trees, but woods. When the train passed over the Yangtze River it was so huge and the visibility was so bad, that from the middle I couldn't see either bank. At Nanjing, there were no cheap hotels for foreigners and I had to pay 200 Y (25 US), or sleep on the street. The Zhong Bei was posher than I was used to, with bell boys in red livery. The smartly dressed receptionist checked me in with a typically automaton manner and a blank expression, then she said 'I can speak German' and wrinkled up her pretty nose; three of them came into my room smiling and showed me the bed, the mirror and whatever else they could think of and we drank tea together. Generally I wouldn't expect to pay more than five US and never more than ten. I put up with the luxury that night and planned how I was going to get to Huangshan tomorrow.

## Wednesday, 18th January

I was up and out by 7am to try and buy a bus ticket to Huangshan – impossible, 'Meiyou' is all I could understand;

it means 'No, don't have'. I got some strange three wheel contraption to the railway station and did manage to buy a train ticket for 11:40. So then I needed to get myself back to the Zhong Bei. There was an argument about the fare and the bloke followed me into the lobby and complained to the staff there. I got my stuff and checked out. The staff at reception were so charming, and they escorted me outside and down the street to the bus stop. I got to the railway station and was in the queue two hours early to get a seat, but by the time it was 11:40 I might as well have been at the back of the queue, as the people without seats just walked to the front. The seats were plywood benches covered with a half inch of foam and plastic. I thought 'hard seat' wasn't so bad, to start with. After three and a half hours, the novelty had worn off and I wished I'd planned my route differently. The bench seats faced each other and were numbered off as three seaters; we had four to a seat and people standing where they could. There was a general mix of people: students, workers and families, all going home for the New Year celebrations. Right in front of me was an older man with his lovely young daughter; she had a classic Han Chinese face, with a cute nose and very appealing eyes. She didn't look so pretty when she was spitting and clearing out her nose on the floor.

After seven hours, I was wishing I had missed this diversion out altogether. There were patches of slush outside and it was raining, it all looked grim and I wasn't anticipating an easy time getting to my destination. I discovered that Huangshan Gate, the entrance to the Yellow Misty Mountains, was 70 kms further than Huangshan city and there would be no busses when I arrived or cheap hotels. Around 7:30 in the evening, the train stopped and I was happy just to be getting off; the rain was of less importance. The people in my carriage were very friendly towards me and several of them helped me to get all my luggage down onto the platform. As soon as I exited the station, a woman met me and led me to a regular hotel for Chinese only. Hotels in this country are regulated and most have no licence to accept foreigners. I was smuggled through a side door and taken straight to my comfortable room, which cost me 70 Y. Then the young daughter of the owners brought me tea and cooked me supper for an extra five Yuan. Jiang Xiao Ling her name is, she told me I was 'beautiful' and instructed me not to come out of the room until they come to get me early in the morning. Okay.

### Thursday, 19<sup>th</sup> January

I left the Jin Lin Hotel at six thirty as instructed, it was still dark and I found somewhere to eat rice gruel and oily dumplings and then waited for the bus to Huangshan Gate.

Two hours on a leaky old bus and I'm now in this cold, damp hotel room; it's nine degrees and I'm wearing six layers of clothing right now, just like the Chinese do. The place is very nice, as it happens, with some hot springs running out of the mountain. There are pine trees, huge boulders and an artistic arrangement of stone paths, bridges and archways. I can't see far up the mountains because there is a low, dense cloud hanging over, giving out a misty drizzle, and often turning to sleet.

### Friday, 20<sup>th</sup> January

I had to take a Daihatsu taxi for 20 Y to the entrance of the national park, and then with my discount card, I still had to pay 40 Y just to enter. I started to walk (having left my two holdalls behind at the hotel). There was a kind of icy snow all around as I climbed the granite steps. They got steeper and steeper and I took several rests, until I realised I had climbed out above the cloud layer. The sun was bright and warm and my first sight of those fantastic peaks was awe-inspiring; jagged spiky lumps of granite rising above the misty white cloud below. It took me two and a half hours to reach the top of the first ridge and it was cold and windy up there. I could see both sides and the views were breathtaking.

I knew I was going to have to sleep up there and had brought my rucksack with everything I needed. A strong wind was blowing and the mountain ranges looked quite inhospitable. Then the sun was clouded out, as were the views, within five minutes of me reaching the saddle where I planned to make camp. I found a snug little alcove amongst rocks and trees, just off the path and I bivouacked there. No tent, I just laid a heat reflective sheet out in the snow and pegged my waterproof poncho down; I propped it up with a tent pole I'd cut from one of the nearby bushes. Two hours later I knew the sun was setting, because the mist all around me had turned orangey, then it quite suddenly went grey. It was no later than six thirty and I had a long night ahead of me. I had stale bread and tinned pork fat to eat and not a lot else, just my harmonica to keep me company.

At first I was plenty warm enough, the inside temperature was about 6°c and my roll mat helped to insulate me. However, the foil sheet caused condensation and by morning my bedding had soaked it all up. It had started raining in the night, not hard, just miserably and the wind howled. I was quite sheltered by the rocks around my site, but the inside temperature dropped to 4°c and if I moved, then the ground sheet would just slide on the soggy, packed snow beneath.

## Saturday, 21ˢᵗ January

I was up with first light (about 6:45), I hadn't slept much, just lain there in a crouching position, trying not to slip off the mat, which was only 18' wide. I broke camp as soon as possible; I had my remaining stale roll, but spat out the last mouthful, as it really did taste mouldy. China is not big on wheat and it was the driest most unswallowable bread I've ever eaten.

The stone cut steps wound all through the jumble of boulders and pinnacles, along the ridges and down through natural chasms. Mostly there were no rails and the wind, coupled with the wet ice underfoot, made the journey risky; I had slipped and fallen into a ditch yesterday with my heavy rucksack on my back. The thick cloud meant I couldn't see too far ahead, or much over the side. I just focussed on the steps and used my tent pole for balance. I had a map (just a hand drawn guide really) and my compass helped me to chose the paths which would take me right across the top of my stretch of mountain; It was as if I was navigating the spine of a dragon. It was several miles of struggle against the elements and it felt like a pilgrimage. Eventually I found the trail that spiralled down the edge of a pinnacle and brought me out from the grey wet cloud sitting over the peaks. I was in sunshine and it wasn't raining, the valley below was green with stunted pine trees and had a white mist lying along the river line. I felt good.

The hot springs resort was based around a cave, supposedly containing hot water pools. I paid my entrance and took a towel, but when I was led through to the pool I couldn't use it. It was a steamy tiled pit, full of naked Chinamen, and I was off, back to the bus stop in my wet clothes. I got back to Tunxi and slept in my clothes to dry them out.

## Sunday, 22nd January

The only tickets available for the train to Changsha were 'hard seat', class without a seat, but I had no choice. I spent two hours on the cold, damp platform, then twenty hours of sheer hell getting to Changsha. I didn't get a seat, but I managed to perch on the edge of a tiny tea table for half of the journey. The floor was wet with gob and people kept treading on my feet. I had to change trains at Yintan, where I got on the next one two hours before it left, so got myself a seat by the window. Suddenly people swarmed onto the platform and rushed the train to get a seat.

Twenty minutes before we left it was completely chaotic. I couldn't believe the amount of people cramming in: it was so full, nobody could move and it was a physical impossibility for everybody on the platform to board. People ran wildly, screaming and shouting from door to door, trying to prise their way in. A woman with a child pleaded for me to open the window so she could get in. I was going to do it, but the other passengers stopped me. People die in these crushes – it's not just the people, but all their boxes and sacks, bashing you in the face or the back of the head. There were shouts and cries of pain coming from the aisle, and I saw a cheaper class of carriage pull in to a stop on the next platform. These were just like cattle wagons, with four tiny open windows for each side and a big sliding door, which when it opened, hundreds of people spilled out from.

Once no one else was getting in, the masses in my carriage settled and found their standing, or perching positions. Some were sitting or lying amongst the luggage on the wall racks. It didn't seem possible, but every hour or so, the train staff managed to force a narrow stainless steel food trolley along the aisle, shouting warnings as they went. Few people had elbow room to eat and most couldn't have reached the trolley either. When we stopped at the minor stations, people wanting to get off had to use the windows: no one could get to the doors.

**Monday, 23rd January**
For the last four hours of this journey I was suffering pretty bad stomach pains, mostly due to holding a cramped position, leaning forward over my bags that I was guarding with my legs; I couldn't see them as I had a bag on my lap too. Of course, I couldn't get any sleep and my legs had seized up, so that when the train finally arrived at Changsha (about 7am), I had difficulty getting myself off it. The ordeal wasn't over, as there was quite a walk amongst about two thousand people trying to file through the narrow ticket exits. I have never been so pleased to pay 30 USD for a hotel room, with air conditioning, a clean bathroom and hot water.

It is much warmer outside than anywhere else in China so far and I had a pleasant walk through town to the Hunan Provincial Museum, where the main exhibit was an unwrapped mummified woman in her fifties, with tuberculosis, gallstones and schistosomiasis. She was entombed 2100 years ago, during the Han dynasty. It was quite an unpleasant sight to view actually, with her soft wrinkled skin looking like a bag of mashed potato. I bought lots of different foods from a street market before going back to the hotel to see if their travel agency had managed to buy a train ticket to Guilin for tomorrow. They got the ticket for me, with difficulty, and for the Chinese price, without charging any commission. The staff there were all great and wanted to practice their English with me, so they invited me to go out and eat dinner with them: it was hotpot, catfish and duck's guts.

**Tuesday, 24th January**

Chen Ying, the receptionist, gave me a morning phone call and then she accompanied me to the train station and made sure I got to the correct ticket barrier. The queue was slow as the guards were searching everybody's belongings for fireworks. This is a big problem in China this time of year and there are horrific posters stuck up, showing the results of massive fireworks explosions that went off in crowded carriages. My ticket was a 'hard sleeper', so I did manage to sleep for half of the eleven hour journey to Guilin, and then I left the train and checked into a grotty, overpriced hotel.

I went out for some street food. Passing a night club doorway, where part of the attraction was dwarfs with Mohawks and very young looking girls in cowboy hats, I was accosted by a couple of taxi girls in trouser suits, who tried getting me into the back of a parked car. This town is a different China to what I've seen, for sure. I got my food and went back to my dingy digs.

**Wednesday, 25th January**

The lonely planet guide book warns 'Guilin is a great place to learn about capitalism'. The bubble has burst and I feel like I'm in South East Asia again, but without the sunshine. I was cheated on the room last night, and they've all tried to sting me on minibus prices. All through China I've been helped by genuine people, but down south it is touts trying to skim something all the time."

I took another nine days getting to Hong Kong, which included holing up in the tourist town of Yangshuo, while I waited out for the Year of the Pig to break. Yangshuo is the place with the lazy sunset river and ridiculous limestone fingers sprouting from everywhere. It was a relatively comfortable place for travellers to congregate, but I'd had enough by the time the incredibly dangerous firework madness was over. Next stop was Canton, by night bus – no more trains. It was a modern sleeper bus, but a bad road. They had loaded it with as many Chinese who wanted to go, so that the sleeper seats were just full of people sitting on them and no one could lie down, regardless of which class of seat you'd bought. It was all a bit more expensive in Canton and quite modern in comparison to what I'd seen. The faces were very different too. Gone were those round faces with rosy cheeks, the people looked more like the lot from your local Chinese takeaway.

I was very amused by the information board on the inside of my door, highlighting the hotel conditions of residence. I had to write it down in my journal to remind me of the behaviour expected of guests. Please see below some of the more reasonable requests:

'Dear guests,

We hope that you will be comfortable and safe during your stay in our hotel. In this case, we will appreciate your co operation in complying with the regulations as follows:

5. All articles in room are for use only, not as memento to take away.

6. Please don't move and dismantle the electric appliances and equipments, otherwise, compensation must be paid according to their prices if there are any loss or damage.

7. You are not allowed to bring in inflameable, explosive, poisonous and radioactive materials, livestocks and rancid materials. You should not cook food, light a fire or fire crackers in room as well as smoke in bed. A fine of 30 FEC will be issued to any violators.

8. Visiting prostitutes, prostitution, drug taking and group gambling in room are strictly forbidden. Violators will be punished according to Chinese law.

9. Please keep your room tidy. Don't spit to the floor, litter cigarette end and ash as well as rind and groceries, pour tea into wrong places. Don't put tea bags into wash basin or billet but dustbin. Don't dump anything and pour water out of windows. If having done so, you will be punished or fined according to the concerning regulations. Please pay attention to your appearance, when leaving the room, don't wrap yourself with sheet and quilt cover.

10. Visitors are required to register at the reception. Those who come to visit after 11:00 pm are not welcome. A couple persons who are opposite sex grown-ups wanting to live in a same room must have a legal marriage certificate.

14. Please write down your good advice on the notebook at the reception. We believe this will help us to improve the quality of services. Thank you very much.'

The last thing I had to do in China was buy the boat ticket to Hong Kong for the next day. It was a long ride down the Pearl River on a slow old tug and took most of the night. I was charged double because it was Chinese New Year. I met a young German backpacker at the boat dock, he had paid extra for the jet ferry, I laughed so much when he said 'I cannot be confronted by another Chinese person, I really can't, I've had it, I can't take anymore.'

# CHAPTER 10: INDO-CHINA LOOP

It is enough to say that I made it to Thailand and did train for three months to become a Muay Thai fighter, successfully surviving my first bout in the Muay Thai ring as a professional. I was in South East Asia for five months all in all. Whilst I was still preparing for my first fight, My old mate Del sent me an aerogramme to let me know he had ditched his factory job back in Kent and was coming over to watch me fight. Once that ordeal was out of the way we would travel on together, eventually making it to New Zealand.

After the boxing match and a fair bit of partying, we took off on a road trip. Starting in Phnom Penh, Cambodia, at the beginning of the rainy season; it was to be a big wide sweep through South Vietnam, Central Laos and North East Thailand.

From the capital, Phnom Penh, we had to get a share taxi down highway one to the Vietnamese border at Bavet/Moc Bai – but first of all, we needed to get from our guest house to the taxi point and all the roads were between one and three feet deep in monsoon water and sewage. Phnom Penh's roads were the most potholed of any city I've known. The water was brown as a cup of PG Tips and you never knew where the potholes you could fit a moped in were. More concerning, was knowing there were broken open drain accesses, with bits of steel reinforcing rods sticking out from them. You knew they were there, but not exactly where.

Two of us, with rucksacks, on the back of a Honda C90 moto-dop (moped taxi), didn't stand a chance. I went out on the back of Sok Sreng's moto and we flooded out on the way to the taxi stop; the bike virtually drowned in the streets around the Olympic Market. Next, I flagged down a cyclo (three wheeled bicycle taxi) and that got me through the water course to the share taxi meeting point. Our ride was a standard white Toyota Corolla and the driver blasted out Malay type music for the whole four hours (I think he only had the one tape) as he drove – fast as he could, on the narrow raised causeway surface that was highway one. Either side of the road were flooded swamps full of lilies and water hyacinth, as well as empty rice paddies, ready for re-cultivating.

Our driver swerved recklessly whenever we met a vehicle coming towards us. If the cars and trucks had slowed down to pass, they couldn't all have done it, because the road didn't have the width to pass safely. It was the momentum in the swing that threw the wheels back onto the crumbling tarmac edge and if both went for it at the same time, swinging straight back quick, then it worked, as by the time the rear wheels left the surface, the front ones were back on it.

Bavet was like a desert of mud to confront Vietnam's green and neatly cultivated land, just a hundred yards or more across a plastic bag strewn wasteland. It was teaming with rain and I slipped and almost went into the open latrine that the friendly Cambodian border guards had indicated as the toilet; it was right beside the road and without any screen or barrier and when I got back to the kiosk, soaked and filthy, they tried to charge me a dollar for use of the facilities.

The Vietnamese border police were anything but friendly, but we got through and were met by a local driver. So we got into the oldest, most battered Peugeot taxi imaginable. The seats were ripped and nothing worked, but it didn't matter to us. We were in 'Nam and on our way to Saigon and the Sinh Café.

We were there a few days and rented bicycles; it was adrenaline cycling on those classic sit up and beg frames. I was rammed into the road by a moped within the first ten minutes, and then nearly run over by a truck. We did get our Lao transit visas (twenty five dollars for seven days!) and were off up country, headed for the DMZ. We trusted in a couple of cyclo drivers to peddle us to one of the public bus stations, shunning the tourist busses that the cafés organised. We ended up miles away on an area of wasteland where people were hanging around. Our cyclo drivers obtained bus tickets for us, cheaper than the tourist bus, yes, but I know we still got ripped off. We had to wait around for a couple of hours until enough tickets had been sold, and then our rickety old bus coughed its way off the site and onto the hellish soot choked road out of the city. Most of the vehicles seemed to be Russian and Chinese trucks, belching black filth, and they were all sounding their horns.

Our bus was a basic affair; we shared a bench seat with other passengers and it was hot and sweaty. The leaky exhaust pipe running under our side made the floor hot and whenever the bus stood still (about every twenty minutes), noxious fumes welled up from where the panelling met the deck. They rarely turned the engine off at stops and we both ended up with bad throats. We had foolishly chosen the sunny side too and the combined effect was punishing. We had to put up with flies, no leg room and people's feet hanging over the back of our seat and pushed through underneath it too. These people were spooks; they just stared at us the whole time, even reaching out to examine the hairs on our arms, as they didn't have any: we felt like zoo specimens. This was definitely not the 'express bus' we had been sold. It just kept stopping everywhere: for passengers, to pay police bribes and for breakdown assessments. The bus kept on all night, apart from a two hour stop at a works yard somewhere, to have its chassis welded up at two in the morning. We were there for three hours and people slept on the bus or just on the ground outside. We made it to a fly infested rest stop at Nha Trang around first light, where everyone went straight to the giant concrete troughs and washed their feet, faces and lower arms. Driving on into the new day - I estimated we were only making an average of thirty five kms per hour - more things went wrong, including the wheel nuts disappearing. We broke down repeatedly, culminating with the driver's assistant removing a part of the water pump system. He flagged down a passing bus and clung to the back of it with the broken pipe section in his hand, disappearing down the road. That was it really, and when we saw some other passengers abandoning the wreck and hailing down other transport we gave up on our fare too.

It was late in the afternoon on our second day on the road; we were riding standing up, in an even older bus with no back door. There were so many people standing that I couldn't even see the seats, we could never have got through to one if we'd seen it anyway, not with backpacks through the crush of people standing. This bus didn't stop too often, but when it did, we were left standing around for ages. So there we were, still heading north, standing on the back steps, hanging onto the rails.

A couple of hours of this shit and we were less than cheered by the sight of our original bus overtaking with horns sounding and the passengers shouting and laughing.

We'd bought tickets to Da Nang, but Hôi An was closer, so we decided to get off there. Apparently it was only two hours away – but it wasn't. It actually took us six and a half hours to reach the turn off and during that time I nodded off a few times while standing in the doorway, so sat down on the floor, hemmed in by people's legs for safety's sake. It got dark and I couldn't have got much lower; the metal step hurt, I had stomach pains and I was seriously fatigued through lack of sleep. After thirty four hours on the road, we were finally dropped off at the Hôi An turn off: an isolated unlit open space. We didn't have much time to worry about where we were, as two riders on Russian two strokes pulled up before we'd walked fifty yards.

After an unfriendly discussion over the fare, we were whisked away before I'd even settled my rucksack. I hung on to my bit of seat for dear life, as they hacked off into the night; I thought I was going to lose my bag several times as the riders dodged potholes and swung round the corners. Del was coughing and sneezing and I had bad stomach cramps. The road was smashing my pelvis with every jolt of that final ten to fifteen kms and I'd had it. The tourist bus from the Sinh Café had been advertised as taking eighteen hours to Hôi An and we wished we'd taken it.

Hôi An was a nice place to rest up, it's true, although two days later Del was in the local hospital, with a drip stuck in each arm. He had contracted bacillary dysentery, probably from all the ice creams and sugar cane drinks he'd bought in plastic bags from the kids outside the bus windows. In the Saigon River, we'd seen kids waist deep in black water, washing out old plastic bags they'd salvaged, so I don't suppose street vendors were buying brand new clean bags.

I recovered quite quickly from the trip, but Del had a bit of an ordeal. He'd been leaking from both ends for a day before I got him to the hospital and was throwing up on water. The bed they gave him was a flat board with just a straw mat on it and the sheet was soiled with traces of blood and other stains. Once the saline drips were in, they left him for three hours with a dirty plastic sick bowl and an old bed pan for company. The place was filthy, with rusty iron bars on the windows, dirty cracked floor tiles, pealing plaster walls and used cotton wool buds left around. The toilet and only washroom just had a filthy hole in the floor and a big water trough with a single scoop.

They supplied a pick and mix variety of coloured pills for me to administer to Del, and that was what you got for your fifteen dollars. We had to go back the next day for another subscription of pills for him and that time we got the boxes too. On one of them it said vaginal suppository. We didn't bother going back the following day. Instead, I took charge of Del's recovery. I prescribed five litres of water to be drunk each day and only one meal per twenty four hours: a small watery bowl of boiled carrot soup. I genuinely did believe that was the best way to wean him back onto food, but it was satisfying too: Del hates vegetables and anything not fried. On the third day, I let him eat a little fish too.

When Del was fit to travel, we hired one of those Russian bikes, a Minsk maybe, to get us to the My Son plateau, an archaeological site quite a way inland. The last bit of the road withered down basically to a dirt track no minibus could have handled. The track dead ended at the site and there was even a bit of a muddy gorge to scramble across; it was great fun and of course there were virtually no other visitors. It is an ancient Cham city, founded around fifteen hundred years ago and set on a wide outlook, part grown over with secondary jungle. The surrounding hills, and some of the ruins themselves, hadn't been cleared of mines from the war, so the trails through the ruins were quite selective. It must have been fantastic, but the Yanks had bombed the hell out of it in the war. It was well worth the visit and the adventure getting there and away. We did China Beach at Da Nang and the Marble Mountains too; I developed a bit of respect for that ugly two-stroke rattle box – it could take a battering.

When it was time to move on, a much better bus took us over the Hai Van Pass and onto the city of Hué, which was the old imperial capital. The journey to the Lao border was disjointed; first we had to get up and out by three thirty in the morning to get a bus which was supposed to leave at four. It wasn't ready to go until six, as they won't leave till they are full to bursting. Despite the argument over the fare and the realisation that we were still getting ripped off, I was quite pleased that they were still using a little old Citroën H for the job; they were first built in 1947. This one had truck wheels, and a lot of the bodywork was made of wood. It was painted up, bright yellow and red, there was no glass in the windows and they'd crammed in so many bench seats that anyone over twelve years of age couldn't sit on them straight, not without their knee caps scuffing the back of the seat in front. The hardwood backs stopped right where your spine curved and your knees had to fit against or above the seat back in front of you. With the rigid chassis and the bumpy road, it was your spine, pelvis and knees or shins that got it. I don't remember how long it took to get to Khe Sanh, but it was quite a ride.

The countryside we drove through was the real deal if you've watched some of the cult Vietnam War films: *Full Metal Jacket*, *Hamburger Hill* etc. This was the heart of the old DMZ (Demilitarized zone), strategic hills and fire bases; we passed the Rockpile and the Dakrong bridge leading to the A Shau Valley. There was a lot to see along the way, like bomb shells stacked by the road for scrap metal collection. I saw one old boy with an entire bomb strapped to the back of his bicycle.

When we got off the bus and our bags were dropped down to us by the bloke who'd been sitting up there, I realised that he had nicked my Maglite out of the front pocket; just another reminder that we didn't need to hurry back to this country to not be treated decently.

Khe Sanh itself was interesting; it had been a huge US combat base on a wide plateau, complete with a runway, bunkers etc. During the Tet Offensive in 68, the base was besieged by NVA (North Vietnamese Army) and Viet Cong; it held out, but proved to be useless and just tied down America's resources for weeks, while major cities in the south were attacked simultaneously. The denuded hilltop was still littered with unexploded shells, mortars and other war crap.

The border at Lao Bao was quite close, but it still took time and agro to get there. As we boarded our last bus, we didn't care about the discomfort of the wooden floor, or that the other people giggled as the conductress ripped us off; it was our last bus in that country and we wanted to leave. It dumped us off two kms from the border and we had to take motorcycle taxis to the Vietnamese checkpoint, which was another argument. Del couldn't stand the Vietnamese by this stage and I was struggling to keep an open mind myself – then the last chance to retain a decent impression presented itself. We'd had our passports stamped out and there were two young girls standing by the kiosk who had drinks for sale, we'd used all our Vietnamese Dong and so couldn't buy from them. Their faces turned instantly from sweet innocence to something extremely unpleasant, they pointed viciously down the track to Laos and told us to 'Fuck off now!'.

We had to walk and sweat the best part of a kilometre in the midday heat to get us to the Lao border checkpoint, and it all changed just like that. The Lao police were friendly and amenable (they did charge us a hundred Thai Baht, but we didn't mind), the female officers' uniform was a green sarong with traditional embroidered hem and everyone was polite and respectful.

We had a local coffee: thick black tar with sticky sweet condensed milk, and made a deal with a truck driver to take us on to Xépôn, only sixty kms, but it took two hours. The road was very bad, but the scenery was nice. There were some hill tribe villages near the road and I got rid of my old tracksuit bottoms out of the window, as we passed by some people who looked like they could use them. We were crossing the heavily bombed Ho Chi Minh trail area and the evidence was everywhere. At one point we saw three boys, right beside the road, proudly showing off a giant aircraft turbine they were digging out of the ground. Another sight was a man and his wife, chest deep in a hole they had dug, with piles of corroded bullets in a heap by the edge of the road.

We had to stop off in Xépôn for the night: a dark, dusty place, just the one street really, with all the shops and homes lit by simple paraffin lamps made out of tin cans with a wicking tube. You could get coffee, but we had to buy tinned food imported from Thailand that evening, as nothing was open after dark. It was amazing how many everyday objects were made from bomb casings, including the piles for stilt houses.

Laos was a breath of fresh air, almost no built up infrastructure and very sparsely populated all the way across to the Mekong River. It was forest and hills, with the odd primitive village, for most of the three hundred kilometres or so. There were no busses on this route and we had to hitch a ride from Xépôn to Savannakhet in a Russian Kamaz truck that was heading west. This was the main road between Vietnam and Thailand, but it was both dirt and broken tarmac; the dirt parts were better on the whole, as the tarmac had so many cracks and craters – you'd think it was alright for a hundred yards, then bang, all of a sudden your spine jarred, as the front of the truck dropped two feet. You had to know it was coming, or be in a constant braced position. That road was unbelievably brutal as it took us down off the mountains to flatten out towards the Mekong basin. The whole area was so totally undeveloped and unspoilt.

Those Russian trucks were tough, as well as surprisingly cramped; the awkward shapeless seats left very little knee room. The truck we took from Xépôn was empty, bar the driver, his mate and two Vietnamese police officers riding in the cab with us. Communications were basic and we didn't understand why they were taking an empty truck to Thailand. They were alright though, and when we got there five hours later and gave the co-driver the five dollars agreed, he handed one back for coffee. That man saved the honour of an entire nation with that simple gesture. We'd almost made it in one go, but during the last part of the journey, the frame of our tail gate shook itself out of position, twisted and then got dragged along the road. Well, we all got out and manhandled the thing round into the open back and lashed it down.

Savannakhet was a large town with a low impact, almost sleepy. It had a market, the filth under foot type and regular shops that sold Thai imported generators and pumps etc.

All foodstuffs we got from the market; I don't remember eating at any restaurants and we just bought food as the locals did. We stayed at the only hotel we were aware of: the Santiphab, a run down French built block just up from the river bank. The river was quite low so we stood on the high bank and stared across to Mukdahan on the Thai side, longing for the 7-Eleven.

There were only a handful of guests at the hotel; they were all Asian, including a couple of taxi girls sharing a room on the next floor. I had just locked our room ready to leave, as a good looking girl caught me in the trap of her eyes while she swayed her hips past me, heading for the stairwell. I played along and let our fingers meet as we walked down the stairs together, just to see Del's face as he waited for me to catch up.

The view of Thailand across the wide river as the sun went down marked the end of the adventure for us; Laos had been an experience, even though we only travelled along one road and were in the country just three days: that time was unforgettable. Twenty odd years later, I realise that I'm looking back at a certain period for South East Asia that no one will experience again. I'm so glad I was there at that time.

The lights from Mukdahan beckoned to us and I know I felt homesick. Chiang Mai in the north had been my home since February and it was June by the time we got back there. Not particularly well off, I decided to enter the ring again and started training for my second Muay Thai shot, but things didn't go to plan. A week later, I got into a fight outside a go go bar, which left me with a broken hand. The upshot was that we put the schedule on hold; I did have that second fight, but not for another four months. We scraped up the money to buy flights back home so I could get fixed and we could earn some more travelling money. The date was set, as we vowed to be back in October to punch it out in the ring, before catching the total eclipse of the sun.

# CHAPTER 11: RUSSIAN ROULETTE

My hand recovered quite quickly, although the third knuckle never came back up; the Thai surgeon described it as 'Policemen's knuckle', as that was apparently a common injury picked up by Thai police officers. Two months after the break, I was out bale carting for a local farm and earning the money for my next flight ticket. In the meantime, I happened across a Convoy of Hope vehicle parked up in a lay-by outside Ashford and got talking. Their next great adventure was a totally new destination: Chernigov, in the Ukraine. The mission was to bring vitally needed aid to hospitals and orphanages catering for those children suffering from the effects of the 1986 nuclear reactor disaster at Chernobyl. Chernigov is the nearest habitable city to the reactor site and many of the people affected were re-housed and cared for there.

Del and I were not so naïve as we had been on that first goodwill mission to the Balkans. It wasn't a case of people's lives depending on us, or that we were even going to change anything for those in need. It was more like, "That sounds like a good cause," and an excuse to drive three thousand miles to give the Charger a last run into the unknown; plus it was bound to be fun, so we were in.

I wrote a journal at the time and had not actually re-read it until just recently, twenty three years later. I was pleased to find that it reminded me, in all the detail that mattered, just how that final road trip had made the impression it did.

Also, maybe why I never did another aid run. I hope that readers following this account now will find it as amusing and readable as I just have. I have edited only some small parts from my original journal, which appeared to be duplicating facts and opinions. The body of the text is as I originally penned it. Some recent reflexions are identified by asterisk.

## CHERNIGOV ^ CHERNOBYL

'This mad and misplaced charity adventure began under the auspices of Convoy of Hope. Del and I (actually I had a hard job getting Del to do anything in preparation) got the trusty White Charger almost fit for the road. We were following the convoy leader, Toney's great mission of universal love: from the people of the world to him. The plan was, we would drive a convoy of desperately needed food, equipment, drugs, sweets and teddy bears to the cancer hospitals and homes for the forgotten children of Chernobyl, who were all dying of leukaemia, just over the river from the smouldering mound of radioactive debris left over from the fire at the atomic reactor in 1986. The reality was something quite different.

We drove the Charger to the warehouse to load up with what we considered suitable, we overloaded her, at my insistence, leaving us no sleeping room at all. This was because I said, if it's worth driving three thousand miles to deliver supplies, I was prepared to be uncomfortable, so that every penny of petrol spent moved the maximum weight of humanitarian aid. The Charger thought I was taking the piss and so did Derek.

We met up with Peter Stammers (from the aborted Sarajevo run), whose co-pilot was Christian Dave from "the attractive green trim" call sign. We had thought David a bit of a bland characterless anorak before, but as the trip wore on, he came out alright. Peter on the other hand, went full circle, from being thought of as a prat before, to a reassessment, on account of us not having really bothered to get to know him, or understand him; then right back to the reassurance that he was even more of a prat than we'd first thought. *Peter was okay really, just very weird.* He bought us both a beer and a Kentucky fried chicken the first night at Ramsgate, as the seven and a half ton hire truck he was driving for Toney needed a wheel changing. Del and I did it, as no one else seemed to have a clue.

The Charger was on its forth mission, with no tax, no MOT, and just an invalid green card (for Western Europe only). They all said it wouldn't come back the first time.

### 1st day on the road 16th September

We had a reasonable sized convoy and about half the people I knew already. Toney's jokes over the C.B. about bears, initially echoed by most people and then just feebly kept alive by Toney, Robin and Bob, became more and more irritating as the days went by. Nothing of interest happened in Germany, except it rained as usual, and Robin's Discovery was "losing power". Toney wanted me to take on Robin's trailer but I refused, so he swapped his full box with Bob, who was driving a Transit for Toney and pulling a breakdown trailer. This "service van" contained nothing, except the women's portable loo and half a dozen jerry cans and water containers. What a waste of fuel and opportunity, to drive an empty van with an empty trailer, all the way to the Ukraine, when Toney's warehouse is full of endlessly donated expendables.

Living space in the Charger was just cramped containment, stuff hurriedly thrown in, with the intention of sorting it out at the stops. It became a disorganised squalor that we just put up with. The mould on the dash soon washed off with fresh coffee spills and the door wells and footplate spaces filled up with domestic junk consumed on the way, so that, just about everywhere we stopped and got out, crisp packets, tins, plastic cups, sugar sachets, tea bags and kitchen roll fell out too.

## Day2      Germany – Poland 17th September

We spent the night in a car park at the old Iron Curtain border checkpoint of Helmstedt – Marienborn on the Bundesautobahn 2. In the morning I did a spin in the car park as a tester and noticed a tick tick tick noise coming from underneath, which got faster and slower depending on the speed of the vehicle. Del drove her around, while I hung on out of the door, looking underneath. It was the hand-brake cable, getting smacked by the prop-shaft studs; could become dangerous, so I tied it up.

We started seeing Trabants, those Cold War two-stroke people's cars. We had heard so much about them when the wall had come down, so it was good to see them. The landscape was still flat when we got to the Polish border. Some locals pointed out that we were losing water; the rad is fine while cruising, but not good for creeping along. Robin gave out vehicle papers to anyone who was around him, but not to us, so it's lucky we didn't actually have to show them.

## Day 3      18th September

Poland was a new place for me, I've looked out the train window at it on my way to Moscow but now I was driving through it. Actually Derek did most of the driving, which suited me, I'd rather sit in the navigator's seat drinking coffee and taking pictures. I kept off the CB as much as possible, as the rapport was such a load of shit. The main road was bleak and basic, often forested on either side, with old women and young men standing or sitting on the verge beside their bicycles, selling mushrooms from their baskets. There would be one, two or three people showing off their wares on tablecloths, spaced at every couple of miles. Insensitive jokes were cracked over the CB by stupid people.

The road east carried old trucks, just like the ones belching black smoke on the highways of Indo-China: same party, same equipment; the politics of motion. There was farmland between the stands of pine forest: potatoes and fields full of hay stacks in sheaves not bales. Also there were semi outdoor stalls at the roadside in places, selling garden gnomes, windmills, wagon wheels etc. There wasn't much else to see, other than wooden sheds advertising "BAR", they seemed to be sort of coffee shops that also sold groceries. It was a hot day and we'd left the rain behind.

## Day 4    19ᵗʰ September

The fourth morning we woke up to a cold, damp day. We were in another hotel car park, but Del and I hadn't slept in a hotel. Uncle George, Big Ray and Lady Breaker had been coming back the other way (I hadn't known they were out too) and stopped by 'cause they saw the Charger. They shared some info about the road ahead. I've been a little curious about why George seems to concentrate on helping individual families, who appear materially okay to me, rather than concentrate on people in dire need. Ray was happy to tell me that the hospital they dropped their aid at in Chernigov was "spotless" and well run. I wondered why they had driven so far, on donated petrol money, to deliver aid to an established modern city hospital that was not in any great need. They clearly believed they had accomplished something so worth while, that it would take the back of a shovel to knock the *holier than I was yesterday* smile off Father George's beamer.

Somewhere south of Warsaw we took a wrong road and had to double back, which cost us time and energy and the bear jokes were wearing really thin by now. Sharon was a fat bird from Reading, supposed to be a reporter and was travelling with Ben, the photographer from one of the Berkshire papers. Ben was alright, and Sharon was actually really nice, but did she overdo it on the CB set!

We made a diversion through some quiet rural places; narrow lanes, horses and carts. There were pretty miserable looking homes with roofing felt on top dotted around. This was a really poor and depressing northern hemisphere country; fifty years behind Western Europe, it must have been grim in winter. We stopped around midday at one of the bars for coffee and sausages, both were really good. The farming I saw was so basic, mostly done by horse and by hand. Crops grew in long thin strips, like England before the agricultural revolution and the cows were grazed on the road verge; they could be, as traffic was light and slow.

The White Charger's guardian angel which had looked out for us all through the previous year, obviously didn't consider Chernigov to be a worthy enough cause: no more than most of us did at the end of it all. Things started to go wrong with the previously irrepressible Transit crew bus. Just minor age and stress related things at first. We got a puncture in one of the rear dual wheels and the main spare was flat, so the old third rate sun cracked one came off the rack as a quick fix. *I should say that after the Croatian trips, I had changed all the good wheels for old rubbish, as I thought she would be sitting in the barn for a year or more. I just never bothered to change them back for this trip, as we weren't going to try and MOT it and with duel wheels on the rear you only need good ones on the front.* We didn't like to inflate this spare too much as some of the splits in the wall were a bit shocking. Del put some insulating tape over the worst one, just for a laugh, it stayed on a while too.

We saw orthodox style church domes and more haystacks as the afternoon passed by, crossing the Vistula River at last. It wasn't until about ten pm that we reached the Ukrainian border.

While we all queued, parked in line at the checkpoint, we had about an hour to while away; with little to amuse ourselves with, other than to discuss whether or not the public toilet block was the most notably disgusting sight anyone had ever seen. You didn't even need to look inside to see the shit, it lead you up the pathway, starting on the tarmac with one or two deposits; the closer you got to the entrance the less space there was to walk. I don't know how thick it was inside the door, I wasn't going in.

We were through the Polish side and waiting at the Ukrainian point, while Toney had gone in to sort out the vehicle forms and we were all bored. A bit of banter started out over the air and it got quite blue. A couple of English lorry drivers we hadn't been aware of checked in (cause it was CB radio and everyone on that channel could hear) so we turned it up a notch and introduced the Russian police women as a subject matter. When a trucker asked who we were, I just blurted out "Toney Budell", it was the first name that came out. Someone said the border guards monitor the CB channels and Valerie came on the air for the first time ever; she was fuming. It wasn't mature or professional, but it was very funny. Clearance was obtained and we drove on into the small hours, on a dead straight, but very bumpy road, flanked here and there by pine forests.

We were bouncing around so much; someone behind us asked if we even had any shock absorbers.

I've never seen a night so full of stars that I can remember, it was really like driving on through an unknown and magical great open space.

### Day 5    The Ukraine    20th September

We arrived at our rest stop at 3am. It was a clearing in the forest beside a huge lake and the road bridge had divided the lake in two. We had been driving for hours, hundreds of kilometres, and I could only guess as to the appearance of the land we were deep within. A wonderful mist rose from the lake's surface and the stars still shone in the cold air.

No one was up too early and we all agreed with Toney that, as we were a day early at this point (due to George's advice on a bridge detour), we should spend the day there at the lake; it would be a pleasant place to rest up.

Most people stayed with the vehicles, but just four curious adventurists (me, Del, Peter and Dave – surprisingly enough) wanted to explore. After the minimum of planning, we set off into the deep, mysterious forest. It was great fun and brought out a childlike spirit in each of us. Peter found himself a staff and we were off to see if we could circumnavigate the lake and maybe come across some exciting wildlife: wolves, bears, bison, who could tell?

After some while we spied an old woman amongst the trees, dressed up as if she was out of a Grimm's fairy tale. She was in galoshes, a headscarf, several skirts and an apron, gathering mushrooms into a simple basket slung across her back. Actually we saw two or three such people out foraging. We veered away from the lake shore to cross a small lagoon where the forest was deep and shady, with lots of moss and unfamiliar flora, but we saw no animals. We were joking about the stories from this part of the world, like Peter and the Wolf, and we started to follow a little track that turned into a trail, taking us up and around a mound. A dog suddenly appeared over the top, barking like mad at us; he was guarding territory and we realised we were near the edge of a small gypsy style camp. Someone came out to hold off the dog, it was seriously intimidating and all us lot had picked up sticks or were clutching knives. That was Christian Dave (wouldn't hurt a fly), Peter of the enhanced psycho-connectivity, Del the dog whisperer and myself, the only one guaranteed to be bitten by any stranger dog.

We thought, after that shock, that we would stick closer to the lakeside and eventually arrived at the wall of a concrete dam, the far end of the lake. We stopped half way along, to drink cans of Spring Ora orangeade we'd brought along, it was the stuff left over from the last Steam Rally boot fair we did the year before. It was then that we met the mushroom woman again; she was friendly as it happened and pleased to have her picture taken. It was still early and the others agreed with me to trek along the little river a bit and see what we could discover.

A little way up, and in a sunny clearing, Peter had a funny turn. He just stood there in silence with his arms out to his sides like an aerial. When he recovered he said he'd been picking up a signal from the stick he was carrying then locked onto a third dimension. I don't like to take the piss out of people's weird ways, and I'm not even saying he was a delusional; he had his eyes closed and was sort of looking up. It was quite unexpected though, and we didn't know whether to be amused or concerned; Del took a picture.

We saw the mushroom woman again and it looked like she was on her way home. Peter had recovered and there was a call from a clear space at the top of a bank. It was a group of workmen, not warning us away, as we thought first of all, but beckoning us over. The old woman was with them and had obviously let them know that there were strange men in their forest. Peter and Dave were not so sure, but Del and I marched right over, so the four of us came up and into their clearing.

They were big and grizzly looking: woodcutters, just like out of the story books. There was a primitive multi band saw that they had up there, which they fed timber through, using a trolley on iron rails. There were five or six of them in all, most were sitting around a wooden bench, having lunch under the saw mill shelter.

We were beckoned over furiously, then they all stood up and made us sit down and take their own bowls of borscht (beetroot soup). It was not exactly hot, and neither was it delicious, but we made a good effort over it so as not to offend. We downed our bowls the simple way, like peasants, as there were no spoons. The wood cutters put some tough bread on the table between us, a few raw onions, tomatoes and some cloves of garlic. They gave us some of that raw salted pork fat which I was delighted to see, as I knew the others would have problems with it. I swallowed mine down with enthusiasm to set a precedent, and then watched them having to eat theirs. There was some stringy pork fat in the soup too, which I made sure everyone ate.

We had water, but that wasn't enough. Down off the shelf came a big glass jar, half full of the roughest home brewed spirit I've ever tasted. We didn't want to drink it; we didn't want to drink the water either, but all risked some anyway, before they chucked it out and refilled our glasses with hooch. We all looked at these full glasses of petrol in our hands, there were bits swirling about in it. Sipping at it wouldn't do, I knew we had to down them in one to satisfy our hosts. Del and I led the way as we wanted to see the other two completely drop out of their shells. The woodcutters watched with great approval as all four glasses went straight down. We fought against our gag reactions while they cheered, and then straight away refilled our glasses; "Oh God" we thought, this was going to be a walk in the woods never to be forgotten.

Our hosts drank also, and then decided that one of them should rush off and procure a better class of poison. He went off on a motorbike while the others kept us where we were. Three of them were called Kola; there was a Vassa and something else I don't remember, all clear memory faded after the second toast. This was great, I hadn't touched any spirits since I threw up on the Trans-Siberian and had vowed never again, but this was a riot. We couldn't speak any Russian except spesibo, pajeluista, da, niet horosa, ploho, krasivo and humanitarna pomoc; they knew Coca Cola and one or two others.

The man on the bike returned with a bottle of Cossack best Ukrainian vodka, and we were quite keen to start on that. We were drunk as skunks inside fifteen minutes but they kept sending people off to get more vodka, more food and more Kolas. The man of the gang went off to bring his young son Sergjo to meet us; he brought more vodka back with him too. The boy was frozen rigid in front of us as if he was on parade and he was told to sing us a folk song. After that he settled down okay. The whole thing was so incredible; I wish I could have remembered it all. I do remember Del urinating over their log pile, for about a minute, as we all laughed. They laughed a lot at how drunk we got so quickly and we introduced them to Spring Ora, Tracker bars and Orbit sugar free gum.

When it was time to go, we all exchanged hugs and

powerful hand-shakes, then they gave us a package of bread, cake and pork fat. We desperately wanted to repay them in some way, so searched around and Peter gave them his sweatshirt, I don't remember about Dave, but Derek gave a quality lock knife that was virtually brand new. I saw that some of them needed new shoes and was sure that someone back at the vans would have shoes packed up amongst the aid, so I invited them back to the camp. Just as well really, as we might not have got there otherwise. Sergjo's dad, with his two sons (one being Sergjo and one Kola), led us back to the main road where the vehicle park was. On the way, Kola showed us mushrooms and berries, food from the forest. It was like an enchanted adventure, striding through a strange but slightly familiar woodland, somewhere on the edge of Europe, and it was the last bright warm autumn afternoon that I would see for a while.

Back at the van park our new comrades were looked on with suspicion and it wasn't comfortable. Toney didn't want to know, and nobody could find any shoes, although I knew we had boxes of them. I wanted to drive our friends back to the dam in the Charger, and then find them something useful. General opinion was against me driving and Del was already crashed out, although I did start the engine and the Duke was going to see me back. I saw them getting in the back of Robin's Discovery with a couple of boxes of food I think, so that was it and I turned my engine off. Yes of course I wasn't fit to drive, but I hated Toney and his gang for undermining me, and I sat in the cab for a long time before the red mist cleared. I can't remember ever feeling so angry for so long. I lay down in the sun when I felt it was safe to get out of the vehicle and I was done.

I remember waking up around sunset and it was chilly. I had a blanket over me that Sharon had put down, she loved to mother people. As the days went by I realised there was a lot of goodness in her, she cooked Del and I a curry when we came round, later on, Peter cooked us another one; it turned out this was because Del had given him the impression that we had no food on board for ourselves.

It was a cold moonless night, the stars were out in complete glory again and Del and I stood and talked with Peter and Dave. Peter (we thought he looked like Nigel from Eastenders) opened up by telling us he wasn't from this planet. He claimed to know that he descended from the star system Sirius at the time of his birth. He proffered to know great wisdom but found it impossible to explain the nature of this fantastical knowledge. When pressed he just said we weren't ready and we were still seeing the universe through eyes that couldn't see outside our self inhibited railway tracks. He still looked like Nigel from Eastenders, so that became his new tag.

Nigel certainly had some knowledge of astrology, but also a deep interest in saving the world and every miserable being that crawls on it. His avowed acceptance of unconditional love, without exception, actually riled me a bit. Nigel was pretty much describing himself as the new Messiah. All that aside, we were pretty pleased we had bridged the ideological chasm between East and West, by the sharing of alcohol. That afternoon alone felt like it had been worth the effort of the drive.

### Day 6    21st September
We woke up just before dawn to a fantastic sight and feel. The first frost, quite heavy too. It glittered on the vans, clouded the windscreens and coated every leaf and blade of grass down by the water side. The frost thickened with the light of dawn before dispersing as the sun came up.

We could hear trucks crossing the bridge with more frequency. They would appear out of the mist, then plunge back into it. We were quite amused by a cat and a dog playing together up and down the bank-side; they got on well and obviously worked the site for cooking scraps left over by truckers.

Once Toney had briefed the group, we were supposedly ready to go and the real day began, with vehicle problems, mostly due to the cold night. For Duke and Chrissy Boy it was a daily morning ritual that continued to the end of the trip. The Duke's battery was always flat and he had to use his small generator to power it. He didn't have a trailer on anymore because his tow-bar bracket had sheared in Poland and the Reading press van was pulling his load for him now. Chris's problem was another story:

Back in Croatia Uncle George had escorted an articulated lorry to Rijeka, and we'd unloaded it at the Sathya Sai warehouse; that was when I first realised I was running with Sai Baba cult followers. *It was a kind of new age messianic thing, based around the personality of an Indian mystic, but there weren't any dreadlocked wasters amongst the family. It was a middle class money thing with a gold ring bearing the sign – and it was a con.* Chris is a Sai Baba worshiper who claims a swami is looking down on him, and Tony is looking out for him because he is one of them too. Chris has been to India to stay at ashrams with his wife, who they say controls his life with her fanaticism. They are vegetarians at home in Dorset, but he eats meat here on these trips. We've heard it said that he enjoys the driving, not just for the feel good factor and Baba karma, but for his own bit of personal freedom and the opportunity to have a drink.

The man has witnessed miracles from the hands of his guru amid crowds of millions, and under mystical circumstances. Things such as jewellery suddenly appearing in the prophet's hands; it's true because he's seen it. *I smelt a rat at the warehouse in Rijeka, where there was a shrine to it all. On the wall behind the simple shrine, there was a framed picture representing Sai Baba, with his fuzzy hair and big round face beaming down with an expression of comfort and benevolence. He was standing behind an image of Jesus, who looked troubled and unsure about something. Baba had his hand on Christ's shoulder, as if to say, "Don't worry my friend, I will show you the way."* Chris is fat, physically repugnant, socially lost, and worships the ground Toney stands on. He is also a keen, but not particularly skilled cartoon artist.

Well Chris's little diesel van wouldn't start (fuel problems we thought), so Robin tried a tow start on it. On the first attempt Toney's tow-rope snapped and Chris's bumper got pulled out of shape, because he put his foot on the brake while being towed at twenty miles an hour. I'd seen the commotion and heard Toney bellowing, Del was just shaking his head. Next they tried a silly extendable towing hook that was doing terrible damage to the front of Chris's van. They had attached it to the bumper again but not even the middle of it. Toney is not very mechanically able either, but also, he just doesn't care; he gets all his vans, trailers and repairs free of charge, or sponsored at least.

I did offer my chain but Toney wasn't listening. I had an aluminium scaffold tube too, but they just persevered. I think the hook failed three times, it was just pulling the bumper away from the front of the van. We cringed as we watched. Toney was yelling "First gear!" and Chris stuck his head out the window shouting back "I am in first gear", while turning the ignition key to guarantee the thing wouldn't start. I stood there holding my own 20' chain (would have pulled it straight from the axel) mouth open while they carried on with the wrecking bar.

Toney gave Chris a humiliating dressing down and hoofed him out of his own vehicle, putting another driver in. Finally it did start, with clouds of black smoke and the front end pulled out of shape. We got on the road soon after and all was jolly again. One of the women had offered up a cover, saying "Oh, Toney's always grumpy first thing in the morning before he's had his coffee", and that was the incident forgotten.

The road was straight, through big open fields, interspersed with woodland. In some fields, huge open spaces because of the collective agriculture policy that hadn't been applied in Poland, there were the biggest haystacks I've ever seen; they were long like terraced houses. There were women performing their daily drudgery out in the fields, potatoes etc. and old rickety trucks passing us the other way, with whole haystacks on board, loaded out over the cabs too. Some of these looked very precarious and I watched a sheaf fall off one, bouncing off the bonnet as it passed us. The road was very bumpy and we had reports from following vehicles that the back of our van was bouncing up half a metre, then almost hitting the road. The brakes were bad enough; we didn't dare use anything but gentle pressure, as it just caused the brake fluid to squirt out from the leaky right hand cylinder, all down the wheel and tyre. Consequently we had to use time and gearing to slow us down, and the hand-brake to come to a full stop. Whenever the convoy had to stop, we would cruise on past them all and pull up in front of Toney, which amused us. *This meant the White Charger was always at the front, leading the convoy when we moved out, he didn't say anything but we know the convoy leader must have been deeply irritated by this.*

An indicator stopped working about this time and the radiator was blowing water out of the overflow at every stop. We couldn't tell anything from the temperature gauge as the thermostat was shot. Still, nothing actually happened to stop us motoring and we came into Kiev about midday.

The capital city of Ukraine was not a joyful looking place. Grey and miserable Soviet housing blocks, people wearing 1970s style anoraks and Terylene trousers. Everyone seemed to have a frown on their face. There were trams and power cables on short pylons, running along the city's main roads. Out of Kiev, we went north for three or four hours. I noticed enormous great bird's nests, built on top of telegraph poles, some two and a half metres wide maybe. I'd never seen stork's nests before, didn't see any storks though.

We entered Chernigov during late afternoon. At the entrance junction stood a big Orthodox church on a green mound (it was actually the roundabout I think), it had a golden dome and was classic Russian style. We arrived at our base hotel, I forget the name, but there was no one speaking English to meet us and it was dark and miserable inside. No one could say whether we would be offered free rooms or if we'd have to pay, and how much. Most of us opted to sleep in the vans anyway, we weren't sure if they would be ransacked if left out there unguarded either.

As soon as we had pulled up, half a dozen boys came running with buckets and sponges, to clean our vehicles for a pittance. Everyone else shunned them and some people even stood there cleaning their own vans. I thought that was a ridiculous show of phoney anti-decadence. The whole group of kids came to the Charger, naturally, it was filthy. Apart from the road dirt, we had been throwing the dregs of our chicory coffee out the windows the whole journey and it was all down the sides. To cap it all, and as a bit of a protest, we had stuffed grass under the bonnet and mushrooms in the tops of the bull bars.

The kids started cleaning before I'd even agreed, but that was okay. They were enthusiastic and really did a good job. Chris scoffed that we'd overpaid them by two or three times, but I didn't reckon so. They got nothing from the others and had to split it all between them. These same kids and their other friends and brothers kept an eye on the Charger, and nothing went missing the whole five days and nights she was parked out there. I think we were the only vehicle that didn't have badges and stickers, flags etc. nicked.

When our hosts did arrive to welcome us: Ivan (the interpreter), Vladimir (the mayor) and Vasil (the trench coated, hook nosed, squint eyed minder/facilitator that the new KGB assigned us), things started to progress. We were subjected to vodka toasts and speeches. We were then treated to the stingiest welcome meal I've ever had. *All I can remember was slices of tasteless cheese, stiff bread and Eastern Europe's supply line of cold sliced tongue.* People were polite about it though and Peter declared it "a veritable feast".

For the first night, I decided to chip in and share a room with Nigel from Eastenders and Dave Cardigan. Bob * he looked a bit like 'the Hound' from Game of Thrones now I think about it * and Ben came round for a vodka supper, which I got pressed into partaking of. And it had started… Peter preached unconditional love, while I came up with hypothetical scenarios to discredit his ridiculous standing point. He wouldn't budge, claiming he would still love me if I stabbed his wife. Dave did his bit and distributed some born again Christian literature: no hard sell, just "read these if you've got time". I don't know where Del came in from but he instantly started berating "all the religious shit these church groups push on people", he didn't know that it was Dave who'd brought them. What a laugh this was turning out to be.

## Day 7        22nd September
Events all seemed to run into each other from this midday; the tour was on.

We drove to the first stop to unload medical gear; it was a disused childrens' home. On the way, I was aware of the knocking noise under the rear axel when we stopped for the lights. I had put it down to bumpy roads so far but something was wrong. I looked underneath and both rear shock absorbers were attached at the top only. The lower knuckles were just snapped off.

It was drizzling as everyone pulled up, one at a time, dug out half their load to get to the medical stuff, wherever it was, and then loaded everything else back up so the next vehicle could do the same. Del and I did the usual and turfed ours out on the drive; re-loaded and then physically carried our medical supplies to the drop point. No one else does this, if they did then we would all have been done in only half the time.

Passers by appeared a little resentful, I thought. Some waved as we drove through the city streets; we waved as a van with some nurses on board pulled in and passed us. I couldn't help but wonder why we were dumping our expensive and highly marketable equipment in this place, which was being run by the police as a warehouse, instead of at the hospitals themselves. Incidentally we learned that this ex-childrens' home had been built or repaired, fitted out and funded by previous charity groups, not so long ago.

Next stop was a home for blind and partially sighted children. It wasn't Great Ormond Street, but it wasn't Oliver

Twist either. It was a bit dingy in there (no more than it was in our hotel) and there were kids there with serious challenges, I think they were the lucky ones, big cobble glasses and expressionless faces. It was okay though. They put on a concert show for us, in a dark auditorium. It was hauntingly good, Slavic music, with an accordion, some piccolo type things and a couple of lads on spoons. They played well and it was good to watch, despite the rigid body postures, or maybe because of it. An older girl, who clearly could see, brought some life to the performance with her singing, we all liked that.

This place put on an early lunch for us, much better than the meagre meal last night. These people served vodka at every table we sat down at, any time of the day; we started to warm to it.

Next stop was the home for the deaf, which I must say was a bloody nice place. Of course the stupid women all walked through the dormitories lamenting at such a cold unloving environment, with nothing to make it personal for the children. I think it would be a nice enough place to live, compared to the Stalinist residential blocks, with their tiny identical pigeonhole apartments, where most of the city population live.

They put on a concert for us too. It was mostly a dance show, performed by (apparently) very happy children. The mistresses had a good motherly type relationship with the kids. The teenagers did a 70s disco type performance, then the younger ones did a wolf and seven kids show, it was great. After the show there was another feast, a fantastic spread, and of course there was vodka. We knocked it back much less timidly this time.

And we were off to the next stop. We seemed to be on the 'best schools in Chernigov' tour. I actually think they were privately funded special schools for kids whose relatives had money. Only the first one I would have called basic, with the kids in charity type clothing.

This new place was a private kindergarten, with better stuff than I had as a kid. I can't see how it could be faulted, but there were some who thought they could justify unloading goods there. Toney made all sorts of promises about what he planned to do for the place in the future. I thought it was taking the piss; well meaning, not necessarily well off pensioners back home had donated what they could spare for this cause.

Toney has to be the one to get in amongst the kids on his own and take over the show. He's good at it, and they like him, but I think it's something he's got that he has to be *the* one. He is a nihilist/narcissist and if someone else is centre of attention, he will break that up and steal the show, usually with his glove puppet act *children's entertainers often seem to have similar character flaws I think, I didn't like watching him to be honest.*

Of course there was a food spread too; an absolute banquet, much better than the crap most of us had hauled out over the three thousand miles we'd come, at great expense, to offer them. Ivan was having a great day and Mayor Vladimir was thawing out nicely. Unbelievably, once we had finished up, we found we were off to the fourth great event of the day. It was certainly a school for privileged children. If we weren't drunk we would have been angry, frustrated and embarrassed. Where were the leukaemia victims of the Chernobyl atomic disaster? *Perhaps the authorities had to show the West how well organised and adequate all their facilities were and maybe they weren't supposed to show us any degrading stuff.*

I don't really remember what happened, or what we were

told as to why we were there; but I do remember Toney sat down amongst the children and sang "I Believe in Angels", he finished it off with a dedication of love and charity, "Om, Om" and pledged a load of aid. We were led to a staff room, for a little supper, washed down with vodka, then entertained in an adjacent dance hall by a couple of musicians with electric guitars. Some of us warmed to it, it wasn't difficult. I got up there with Dave Cardigan on guitar and we did "Blowing in the Wind". After that, with the two locals back on their instruments, I did that other great rocking, but lesser known, Bob Dylan number, "Honey Just Allow Me One More Chance". Now it was all livened up some of us had a go at Cossack dancing, it's very tiring. We were blind drunk, Ivan was having a bloody good time and some of the female staff were getting quite keen. Toney was losing his control and it showed. What he didn't like was that all day he'd been grabbing the limelight; whenever someone lifted a camera he had to dive in and hug some children, it was all about the Toney B show.

All of a sudden, we were told we had to go 'cause it was discovered that local kids were in amongst the vehicles swiping things. Toney lost his spot lights, flags and Ford badges; it put him in a pretty foul mood.

We got back to the hotel alright and everyone sort of hung out, resting up against the vans and talking. We were all in good humour, except for Toney. He wanted everyone to go to bed and picked on Sharon, ordering her up to her room. He was right out of order. It didn't help when Del dropped a bottle and it smashed on the road.

So half of us went up to Sharon's room, drank vodka and had a good round of discussion about the whole set up. We came to the conclusion that the staff at these homes would likely be taking a lot of the stuff we'd brought – home with them. We just couldn't see them opening up a hundred standard sized tin cans of assorted western type foods, and then stirring it all up into communal meals for a start. Then there were the crates and crates of plastic cinema style carton drinks, that we all seemed to have brought. Regardless of good intentions, most of us were not bringing out desperately needed humanitarian aid for cancer ridden Chernobyl victims.

## Day 8     23rd September

After the standard measly breakfast of sliced tongue, everyone else went off with Ivan to visit the city museum and the big gold domed church. Del and I stayed back, with the van on a truck ramp and removed our broken shock absorbers. One of the mayor's drivers was sent back to pick us up in the state Lada and bring us to meet the others at the vodka factory, they didn't want us to miss that bit of culture. It was certainly an experience not to be missed.

We were first shown the bottling plant and where they put the different labels on. Then it was off for the banquet laid on in the staff room. They had worked hard and prepared a kind of East West fusion. Slow cooked cheese burgers and onion rings, there were chips and pizza slices as well as a sumptuous salad, and much more. We were just about to start, waiting for Sharon to open a bottle of champagne. Then the cork exploded out and smashed one of the glass ceiling panels, showering the burgers and chips with shards of glass. Sharon was a bit shocked, especially when she found her finger was bleeding. They took her off for some medical care and by the time she came back we were trying every variety of vodka they produced and toasting to whatever ideal any idiot chose to put up. We all liked the brown coloured Ducko vodka the best.

Of course we were all drunk very quickly. Ivan was in his element, but Vladimir and his personal aid, Nikolai looked as if they were not quite sure things were under control. I don't know how many glasses we downed in one, somewhere between eight and fifteen I'm guessing. I do know we ate all the chips and burgers though. The two female line supervisors hadn't had such a good time for, well, maybe ever. The one called Natasha (that Bob quite liked) with very blonde hair, sang a folk song, as did the other one too. Toney and Valery did a duet "Where Have All The Flowers Gone", then as a group we managed the Negro spiritual "Swing Low, Sweet Chariot". The others only knew the first verse so I raced it up going solo with "I went down to Jordan and what did I see", clapping and foot stamping. We had the Banana Boat Song, "Dayo, dayayayayo", and many more classics. Chris and I finished the party off with "Pack Up Your Troubles in Your Old Kit Bag". The little charge hand woman was singing and dancing away, she wouldn't stop. Then we had to go off and visit two kindergartens.

As we left the room, half a dozen of us pillaged the tables for unfinished vodka bottles; including people you never thought would do that sort of thing. Chris was filling up his camera bag with it while telling us to "Shut up". The factory manager was handing us all souvenir bottles of vodka as we left anyway.

Del and I had to get in the back of the mayor's Lada, it had tinted glass and red velvet upholstery. There were stacks of vodka bottles in the seat pockets and on the floor, some of it was there before we got in. You wouldn't think it could get worse (or better), but it did. What the locals must have thought of us, we were an utter disgrace as some of the first cultural ambassadors for the West, we'd have been ashamed if we could have stopped laughing.

The first thing I noticed on arrival at the first kindergarten was Chris's van left crashed into the low brick wall by the entrance. It wasn't clear if he'd done much damage, as the front was messed up anyway, but he'd hit the wall and just left it on there. We caught up with the others walking up an external stairway to somewhere and Chris's trousers were hanging low, showing his boxer shorts. Del yanked them out a few inches so it looked stupid, and he didn't even notice!

I don't remember too much about what we were supposed to be doing there, there was some kind of kids' show I suppose. Sharon was looking after Chris, who was throwing up in the toilet with the door wide open, while the rest of us were being shown through the nursery. Ivan was on the kiddies' exercise rings, Bob and Robin were on their hands and knees playing with wooden toy trucks and Duke was karate chopping a baby doll in its cot. We had another feast laid on and more vodka can you believe it.

Duke disappeared for a short while, then came back in, dressed in full country and western gear. A gun-shot rang out through the whole building and some of us rushed into the corridor to see what had happened. There was Mayor Vladimir holding Duke's smoking six shooter. It was unreal. I'm assuming it was a blank firing .45 because Duke offered us a game of Russian Roulette. So a bunch of us sat around a table in one of the classrooms and he spun the pistol. The bastard thing pointed to me and I was arguing the toss about the rules of this game, while they were all telling me to pull the trigger. Fortunately one of the Ruskies intervened and we had to leave. I was pleased about that.

So roll on the final kindergarten. Chris just managed to get down the steps again before projectile vomiting against the side of the building. He was leaning against the wall and it was gushing out, in full view of the mayor, his cohorts, all the kids, their parents, the staff and any bystanders from the nearby flats who'd come over to see the British humanitarian volunteers. David and Sharon got Chris to his van and someone must have driven it (he didn't have a co-driver), as our hosts led us to an edge of town fuel station, where everyone could fill up. Chris was there at the pumps, he was on his knees, holding onto the open door and heaving.

Time for the next show, and this one was the best. The banquet was all laid out in the dance hall. The kids did really well with their traditional dances, the costumes and all. The food was great with individual clay pot stroganoffs to start with, while the speeches went on. I don't think there were many people actually listening to what Toney was saying; they were just clapping on cue. It didn't matter anyway; most of us had dropped the pretence that we were helping anyone in need.

What made this one the best was that there were bloody good looking youngish women there: staff who were staying for the dance, maybe some of the mothers, I don't know. There was Cossack music and dance; then the lights went low and the slow dancing started. The women were game and all us blokes were ready to fight over the best four or five of them. I think happily married, good Christian Dave was the most disappointed when Toney shouted his excuses for why we had to go. "Right now". We had to drag Dave away; he kept wanting another kiss goodbye. We were gutted about leaving right then, but it probably was for the best, Del and I weren't married (didn't even have girlfriends) but most of the other blokes were.

Outside we had to fight our way to the vans as we were mobbed by what probably was hundreds of kids. We gave out Mars bars and they were like sharks in a feeding frenzy.

Once back at the hotel, the only thing for it was a piss up

in Sharon's room. We all got out the vodka we'd collected earlier. Ben and I discovered we had swiped several bottles of water by mistake.

## Day 9        24<sup>th</sup> September

Today was a different kind of Chernigov experience. While the others went off a bit further afield, Del and I were left behind with the van. It was promised that a mechanic would come and fix it. Vasil's driver did come and suggest that he take the shocks away and weld them up. I didn't think that was ideal, especially as the bits didn't even fit together anymore. So we were left to our own devices.

Duke came up trumps and let Mary go with the others while he kept us company in his motor-home. We were just tinkering around outside when this bloke called John, who was an English ex-patriot, and his wife Neenah stopped to talk. John was ecstatic because of the flags etc. He seemed very homesick and told us he had worked for the diplomatic mission and Neenah had been his interpreter. He warned us repeatedly about personal security and was very protective about his wife's. They said they were going to pop to their home nearby and promised to return with gifts. They were back quite quickly and did bring gifts: a litre of vodka and some chocolate.

So we sat in Duke's van, around the table and drank the litre of vodka between the five of us. The Duke became more relaxed and jolly, while John became more erratic and paranoid. It was all about Neenah's safety but she just rejected his control and latched onto the Duke. She was wearing his cowboy hat and hugging and kissing his cheeks. Then when Duke produced his six shooter and suggested a game of Roulette; John wanted to leave. Neenah took her coat off, saying "I think I would like to dance". It was a terrible situation, John was shouting at her that we were "fucking crazy" and she was a "fucking stupid fucking bitch", then he slapped her. She hated him and was going to stay, he loved her but wanted to kill her, and Duke made the coffee while Del calmed her down and I tried to talk some sense into him. It didn't work and we had to chuck them out, whereupon she squatted in the middle of the road like your neighbour's dog. They both apologised and promised to come back the next day, sober, then they walked off arm in arm and we never saw them again. Once they had gone Duke said "I was getting a hand job under the table". I had wondered why he'd not been in a hurry to get rid of them.

Well we went back in and Duke got out the West Country Scrumpy. We drank that and listened to some stories he told about WW2 escapades in Malaya. He showed us a scar where he said he'd caught a bullet in the calf while riding as a motorcycle dispatch rider. After the war he was an RAF pilot, hence the Red Arrows stickers on the front of his van. One thing got cleared up, and that was his title, the Duke of Somerfield, no one used his Christian name, most probably never asked. The title was a stage name he'd adopted when he took up with the country and western scene. Everyone seemed to assume he was an eccentric landed gentleman, and that's fine; he was a good man, with bowel cancer, spending his last years travelling around with his dutiful wife Mary, taking life easy, but still rolling. Duke was no liberal, and he was absolutely adamant of a woman's place in life; a good man all the same. He knew Toney was a confidence specialist (actually he used a different expression) and told us that the man had been thrown out of the Sathya Sai Baba sect; what for we don't know. When I first started all this, I had no idea it was all run by people involved in this Indian cult; all the inner circle were affiliates it seemed, and Duke wasn't the only one with cancer either. Looking to your last season on the planet must be a powerful incentive to try and get something good done.

## Day 10        25<sup>th</sup> September

After another evening of vodka and discontent, in Sharon's room, even Toney's friends said it wasn't right that he was refusing to put our van on his empty trailer for the trip home.

In the morning I said I wasn't driving it in its current state, so all our gear was unloaded and distributed into the other vehicles that had space. Toney's response was 'How are you going to get home then? You drove it all the way here'. The convoy went out again, leaving Del and I with the van, still on the lorry ramps. We waited for Vasil and his driver to turn up and take us to a car breakers market. It was a great place and they had loads of spare shocks, none to fit a Transit though. All sorts were being sold and I did wonder about the chance of off-loading the Charger there.

Vasil took us somewhere to buy a cassette tape of traditional music, then he bought some heavy bread, raw pork fat and vodka. On the way back, they both stopped at their own homes to deposit gifts they had received from Toney's aid selection. When we got back to the hotel car park (it was actually the side of the road that our vehicles were using) the driver disappeared with the Lada; so we were left standing there with this strange character in a trench coat, with breath like rotten flesh and an expression as if he had worn a monocle during his twenty years in the KGB.

Well there was nowhere to go, except in the back of the van. So there we are, sitting on packing, in the back of an old school minibus, smoking cigarettes and knocking back tin cups of vodka. We did have salt to go with the pork fat (it dehydrates you and helps to get you drunk quicker) we didn't much care by now and certainly didn't want to see any poor young leukaemia victims, not that anyone was going to.

The whole thing was a sham and everyone knew it. The thing that was worrying Del and I was that we had a flight to Bangkok on the 2nd or 3rd of October. I had a boxing match to get through a week later and I'd not been training. Once that was done, we had to get ourselves to the Angkor temples in Cambodia to catch the total eclipse of the sun. Were we going to make it?

Vasil left and we made coffee and ate the rest of the bread. The car wash kids turned up and I gave them loads of apples that I'd brought from home. Then this man and his wife came up to us. I forget his name but his wife was Natasha and they were staying at the hotel. They absolutely insisted that we go up to their room to eat and drink. We didn't really want to, but there was no arguing with the bloke, he was massive, and they would have been terribly insulted if we hadn't.

So there we found ourselves in a hotel apartment with a strange Ukrainian couple we knew nothing about and who spoke no English at all. They were a long way from home, but working here I think. It's strange how you can figure things out and get an understanding, without knowing the language. So out came the vodka and the raw salted pork fat. We very quickly became completely inebriated and so did our host, whose chair broke under his weight. He wasn't even fat, just huge, so he laughed and threw part of it across the room. We started singing songs and so forth, Natasha was having a go at him so we settled down a bit, then made our excuses and left.

We came down into the reception (no idea what time

it was) and found ourselves surrounded by well dressed Ruskies. It seems there was a party in the dining room for the nouveau riche, they certainly didn't look like communists. We got invited to join their formal dinner, and Derek got to make the first public speech of his life. It turned out that these very friendly people were border police officers and their families, the women were knocking back the vodka to shame us.

Del and I were underdressed and unshaven, but we weren't inhibited. Del was getting friendly with a policeman; he was respectable, intelligent, educated and rich. I was trying to get friendly with someone's wife, who was all of those things too, as well as having great legs under her Ra-Ra tube dress. She left me way behind in the bottoms up stakes, and it's a good job I didn't get a chance with her on the dance floor, as she told me it was her father's secret policeman's ball. Seventy years of communism hadn't bred any equality, I could see that. Another thing I could see was Toney and Bob, just walking in with big smiles, as if they thought this was a goodbye celebration and they were just walking into it. They were quickly approached and asked to leave, it was brilliant.

Toney's pride was hurt, and he had Vasil come in and announce that we were tired and had to be up early in the morning to leave. Leave how? Vasil had told me earlier that Chris's van was now on the trailer, for no other reason than that he didn't know how to bump start it. I knew this was so that Toney could say the trailer wasn't available to help us get home and it looked like we might be trundling back across greater Europe with no brakes, no shocks and one indicator.

I confronted Toney and his answer was "Chris is on the trailer because you've got an engine and he hasn't". I left it at that until we got outside so that everyone could hear what was going on. There was a bit of a communal hoo-ha out in the street and pretty much everyone agreed that it wasn't safe, or right, to let us bounce our way across the German autobahn, in the rain with no brakes. Del told him what he thought of the whole shoot; Toney shouted and flounced and Valery said "It's been a long day".

Back in Sharon's room, a load of us got together, drank vodka and argued. It was the last night in town and people were getting stuff off their chests. Bob and Robin came in, Robin's wife (I think this was the first time we'd spoken) was with them to assure us that everything would be alright in the morning.

### Day 11    Leaving Chernigov at last   26th September
I didn't ask Toney again about a lift, I was prepared to get home on springs and I knew the Duke would stick by us.

Toney made the decision that he *would* get Chris's van started, and so we loaded up the White Charger onto the brand new aluminium vehicle transporter; it only just fitted on. The front wheel nuts fouled on the trailer boards so we planked under the wheels to raise them enough.

After a farewell breakfast of tongue, there was Toney's speech, "We came here bringing love, and what we found when we got here was so much love" bla bla bla, he finished it with "I love you" in Ukrainian; what a load of crap. Ivan did his speech, and then we were all given presents. I got a matryoshka doll, or whatever you call it, actually that's exactly what I wanted. The atmosphere changed just like that and all the tension and animosity was gone. The bastard still made me pay petrol though.

As we came out of the hotel, Vasil came running up in his Columbo coat with wild eyes, he presented me with a pack of post cards; he was really pleased to have got them to

160

me. So we hugged each other, and then all the officials too. If we'd brought nothing else, Vasil and the driver had had a good few days out of it and we'd become mates. Del was met by the three main boys who had been looking out for the van, they presented him with a small gift, I forget what, but it was quite touching. They had been around every day, to make sure no one interfered with the White Charger.

I got in to ride with Chris; I forget who Del went with. I put the Slavic music tape on as we were being led out of town to the Chernigov stone and soviet statue. We posed for more photos, said final goodbyes and we were off into the sunshine. Outside Kiev, Chris changed the music and it was Sai Baba mantras, loud and soothing, Omm... He claims that's what keeps him awake on long drives. Actually his van is a shrine to the sound of the universe. I opened the CB mike for about a minute to pump his sounds out into everyone's cabs, just for amusement and so the regular people could hear what I was putting up with.

Chris appeared to be developing a heavy cold and I didn't need to be taking that with me to Thailand. We stopped at the lake again and it was a bloody freezing night, noticeably colder than it had been seven days ago.

## Day 12    27th September

The latter half of yesterday had been slowed down considerably by the Duke's Iveco. He had bought a jerry can from a garage earlier in the week, filled it with diesel, and then put it in his tank. It must have been full of dirt as, ever after, his engine was suffering from fuel blockages when he went over forty or fifty miles an hour. We had tried everything, but it seemed impossible to just drain the tank and start again. We tried battery powered pumps, hand pumps with different sizes of tubing. I even tried the old

161

direct siphon method, but got little more than a mouth full of filthy diesel.

The other incident I should mention is that Toney's brand new super trailer basically started to snap in half. It wasn't man enough to spread the weight over the central suspension bridge, plus the frame and base were all aluminium, so once it got a whip on over several hours, the weak points started to fatigue and crack. We managed to clamp it together with Robin's brains, Del's brawn and my supervision; using whatever poles and bars we could gather together amongst us. Toney didn't have a clue; all he can do is talk. He let us get on with it though, and didn't make a fuss. I would have been unhappy if it was my trailer.

Driving out of the Ukraine we sailed through border control and Bob suggested that Del and I attending the border police party the night before might have something to do with it. Toney disagreed; he thought the growing reputation of British Humanitarian Aid probably greased the wheels, maybe it did.

There were herds of horses and cows in some fields but nothing else new. It was late in the afternoon and we came off the main road to a small town, looking for fuel and a place to get Ford parts. We were told there was a motor factors in Lublin, five kilometres or so down the road, but it closed at five and it was 4:45pm when Chris shouted at people for wasting time at the petrol station. He and I drove around Lublin; we went from industrial estate to motor factors and then found an actual Ford dealer. The shop was right outside town, amid farm fields where people were digging beets. It was the most unusual place to expect to find a Ford dealers and they only had a very small selection of parts, but they had shocks for a Tranny. We raced back to where the others were and Chris sent the triumphant message back "Mission successful, we have the shock absorbers". Still no brakes but you don't really need them in a convoy.

Del and I fitted them, while the Duke was getting his tow-bar welded back on. I managed to smack my broken knuckle when the spanner slipped off a nut, then I scraped my backbone on some projecting edge whilst getting back out from under. Del stood up underneath the open back doors and held his language as tight as he was holding his head.

Before we got back on the main road I wanted to test the handling; we'd topped up with water, brake fluid, oil and petrol. She was damp and dirty and a total mess inside, but she had suspension damping. I stopped outside the gates of a grim looking memorial. It turned out to be Lublin concentration camp. Black and twisted spiky iron railings and a huge grey tombstone-like stack at the end of a long wide empty pit. The roadway passed either side of this to reach the gates, and black birds (crows I suppose) perched on the stones broke the stillness as they took to the damp grey air. I looked down across the broad empty grass field and could see the barbed wire fences and control towers. I could see there must be some kind of a museum the other side of the field, alongside other huts and a group of people were looking around. It was quite a distance away and the gates our side were closed, with no signs up. I turned and walked back to the van where Del was waiting and we got ourselves back to the car park just in time to line up in convoy.

Then we drove, and drove, in the rain, into the night. We slept 160 kms from the border point Świecko. It was a cold night.

## Day 13     28th September

We finished Poland this morning and by the time we made the gnome stop, we were all in better spirits. Before we left the country, we just had to browse through one of these roadside stalls that sell garden gnomes, windmills, riding boots and other weird stuff. I bought a working spinning wheel and a wild boar's head on a wooden shield.

The last ten miles to the German border brought some interesting conversation out over the CB. It was the middle of nowhere, but not far from the Steam Massage building, which itself was miles from anywhere. Suddenly we were running through a gauntlet of roadside prostitutes. There were no buildings around, just trees and heath land. One or two were standing either side of the road, at about one to two hundred yard intervals, stamping their feet in the chill air. I'd never seen this before; it had been dark when we drove this section a week past.

To pass the time on the drive, Del and I did the old window cleaning trick, where the passenger climbs outside through their window, holding onto the roof bars and cleans his half of the screen. Then the passenger takes over the throttle and steering wheel, while the driver goes out of the opposite window to clean his side. Then the CB came alive "White Charger, who is actually driving your van?" That takes people's minds off the roadside scenery.

We got through the border okay and it started raining in earnest. Del and I thought we might just get back home by tomorrow, but before long we were stuck in a horrendous tailback near Magdeburg. It was one of these situations where you sit for ten minutes, then move a hundred yards. We were held up in that for six hours, the pollution was bad, and as it got dark, we started to worry that we might not get back in time to pack before our flight.

**Day 14    29th September**

We'd lost a lot of time and didn't make the planned night stop. In the morning we were on an A road somewhere and everyone wanted to stop for fuel. The first place we stopped at got filled up with vehicles so the Duke, Tim in Chris's van (he was zonked out in the Duke-mobile), and ourselves drove on two hundred yards to the next one. I'm pretty sure the others knew we'd gone on. So we filled up and stood around talking. Then just like that, Toney's convoy roared past at 70 mph; no warning announcement, nothing. Duke said "What the hell" and I would have liked to stay back and trundle home with them, but we just had to get back for our flights and couldn't risk it. As much as we may have despised Toney right then, we needed him to smooth over any hurdles we might come across with officialdom, and we needed to keep a sight on that trailer. The Iveco with its fuel tank problems couldn't tow us any distance if we needed it.

We didn't even get chance to say goodbye, just jumped in and screamed off after the disappearing convoy. We knew they'd never catch up and I think Toney had seen the opportunity to leave the problem vehicles behind.

**Day 15    30th September**

I slept while Del drove, actually he did most of the driving back and I only took over when it was clear he was getting dangerous. You get into a trance-like state after about twenty hours. You think you're alright and that's the danger, 'cause you know you're fine.

**Day 16    1st October**

Well that was about it really, apart from a run-in with some officious German police officers at a fuel stop, demanding papers I didn't have. Then there was us getting held back by a French army patrol just before Dunkirk on the last night. The whole convoy had cruised past the check and we were lagging behind a bit to leave some space as we ran down through the gears. But we were empty in the back, apart from a spinning wheel and a boar's head, so they let us on our way.'

There were decent people on that trip, and I'm sad to say we never saw or heard from them ever again.

# CHAPTER 12: RED DUST ROAD TRIP

I had three days grace before Del and I flew to Asia and an uncertain future. I went to see my grandad; I knew it would be for the last time. Mum and I took him on a little drive in the country, in his little old Mini van, the one we all used to go off for picnics and trips out in, back in the seventies.

I stored the mini away in the boat barn, and then reversed the White Charger into my original barn, breaking another rear light in the process. It was a big step I was taking, bigger than any before. When I'd left on the train, the previous December, I'd planned the trip to last a year and a day, and no more. During that six months away, I'd lost both my grandmothers, Anthony Keeble was gone too, Warren had passed away even before that and I'd missed all of the funerals due to my obsession with travelling. This time, I was going off to live and work where the road took me, and I had no plans to return until I'd made my fortune in the world. I said goodbye to my parents, the dogs, and my cat, the one that used to sit on my caravan step. It was raining the day we left.

Revelation Chapter 17, verses 3-4

So he carried me away in the spirit into the wilderness. And I saw a woman sitting on a scarlet beast which was full of the names of blasphemy, having seven heads and ten horns. The woman was arrayed in purple and scarlet, and adorned with gold and precious stones and pearls having in her hand a golden cup full of the abominations and filthiness of her fornication. And on her forehead a name was written.

## MYSTERY. BABYLON THE GREAT

The solar eclipse over Angkor Wat was a portent. We should have seen it and got out, before we learned to hate that country as much as it hated us.

To start with, we loved the jobs we soon landed as English teachers; it was great being respected there and we genuinely wanted to make a success out of the country. But it wouldn't let us. It was the rest of the shit we hated: the filth and corruption, violence, abuse and apathy. It was the apathy that burned us out and we both developed our own coping mechanisms. I'm not ready to tell that story yet: when I am I'll write a book on that alone.

During that year and a half I was away, I'd spent two months working and travelling in New Zealand, where the road trip continued with me hitch-hiking around the South Island between jobs, before moving on to Australia. Two weeks into that country, and I was sleeping rough in the desert, Uluru (Ayers Rock), with its red glow at sunset, was just a mile away. It wasn't an easy night's sleep for me; more accurately, it was a series of foreboding dreams – dark clouds and burnt paper, dirty scissors and bad blood – it wasn't the experience I wanted: it was a warning, as well as a guilt projection of some things which needed putting right. I was woken just before dawn by the howl of a dingo, and the sky beside the rock was a red glow.

In the morning, I was back in the main square by the car hire centre. I had spoken to three Germans the afternoon

I arrived, about hiring a car and driving to the rock and around the Olgas (Kata Tjuta), the Aboriginal monuments that the Aboriginals themselves ask people not go up to. I didn't know, before I got there, that there was going to be this spiritual dilemma and I had decided not to climb on the rock as my concession, but I *had* gone there to see it. As I had no accommodation or money for breakfast, I was there early and it was just me sitting at the pick-up point waiting for the Germans to show up. A big old classic Aussie car (Ford Falcon Station Wagon) with roo bars and a surf board on top drove by and stopped near me; one of the two Swedish back-packers in it leaned out the window and asked me if I was going to Darwin. Well – yes, but not right now – I hadn't got to the rock; I'd come right to the middle of the red continent to see this thing, on a one way ticket, with no exact plan for how I was going to get out and I needed to see it. I dismissed the offer, and sat back down as the car did a circuit of the square and then stopped in the middle, engine still running and about to leave. Just then the Germans turned up and I made a split decision, heaving on my pack and running for the Swede's car shouting 'Okay I'm coming'.

First stop was King's Canyon, a massive dry rock gorge, with cool shelter, trees and vegetation, and some pools of water hidden in the narrow headway passage. It was an unexpected attraction, two hundred miles from any other notable features, like a version of the hidden gorge in *Mad Max, Beyond Thunderdome*; something that got left behind two million years ago when the land dried up.

The Aboriginal way of life was simply a day to day existence out there; we'd see isolated family communities, built up round a petrol station, where there'd be a couple of rusted old saloon cars, a weather vane and a basic shop under a tree, where the locals would sit around. Semi feral dingos and snot nosed kids with wide eyes and hair bleached like old straw from the sun would wander to and fro. The women had thin legs and pot bellies and the men were shock haired and bearded. One bloke in ragged shorts, pushing his pickup away from the pump with his family in the back, nodded to me in acknowledgement. It struck me that I wasn't looking that much different myself at the time, it sort of felt good.

We drove on to join the Stuart Highway and got into Alice Springs after dark. We didn't see anything of it, as we just filled up on petrol, had an ice cold Coke and were gone. We stopped just north of Alice at the tropic of Capricorn monument; it was a large globe, like an iron cage, supported quite high up off the ground by a steel arm. Oska and I climbed up and got inside it, rocking around like howler monkeys while Tolban took flash photos. Job done, we bumped the car and drove off laughing. The Falcon (nicknamed Sharkey, because of the surf-board fin on top) had a starter solenoid problem and it wouldn't go on the key: it wasn't just for the ninety dollars petrol share that they needed me along.

We passed a picnic park sign and thought it would be a good place to pull up for the night, but stalled the car in the middle of the road doing the three point turn. It took all of us to get her lined up for the downhill bump and while we were halfway through, we heard the low grumble in the distance. 'Road train!' I'd never seen one of these before: huge sixty two wheeler Macks, pulling three or more 'dogs' (trailer units). They're not going to do an emergency stop. Sharkey nearly went off the edge in our panic, but we rescued her just in time. Those trucks are awesome, we got woken up at three in the morning by the thunderous roar

170

and whoosh of another one while we were laid out on our stone picnic slabs.

Dawn brought a fiery red to the landscape the other side of the road and a full moon was setting behind the scrub bushes opposite. It didn't take long for the flies to wake up either.

Barrow Creek was a little outback station where we stopped for fuel, it had some character. There was a wind turbine the other side of the road and then an Aboriginal site; they were living in old caravans and under tarpaulins, beaten up old cars just sat around and it looked rough, like a pikey site back home, but friendlier.

Next stop was the Devil's Marbles: giant red granite boulders, some being five metres in diameter, strewn across a wide valley. According to the 'Dreamtime' legends of the local people, they are the eggs of the mystical rainbow serpent. I've never experienced flies like it; sick of batting them off my face, I thought I'd try ignoring them, while I walked around the piles of rocks artistically balanced on other rocks and slabs. They were in my eyes and round my lips and nostrils; when I felt them getting into my ears, that was enough and I was flapping like a good'n. There were hundreds around, everywhere I moved to, ready to suck the sweat off anyone out in the open.

The scenery from the Marbles to Tennant Creek was even stranger; it was largely flat, but sprouting with millions of metre high termite mounds, looking like spears hidden amongst the small trees and tall grasses. As the day drew on, the land got stonier and the termite mounds changed from a reddish colour to light grey. After Tennant Creek it all got greener, the spinifex grass either disappeared or was hidden by other grasses. It became more and more humid, and then we ran through the first light rain. It felt good with the sticky feel of the tropics increasing; I knew I was getting closer to where I was heading to: back to Cambodia, via the Indonesian archipelago.

I had left Del back in Bodia, just before Christmas ninety five, it was the third of April when I'd crossed the Capricorn line. I reckoned Del could hold in there another month or so. I did feel some guilt at having left him there; I had taken three weeks out of my teaching job for a Christmas getaway and bought a Saigon, Bangkok, Phnom Penh promotion ticket, with a quick jaunt up to Chiang Mai thrown in. I just didn't want to spend Christmas in Cambodia. Once in Chiang Mai, I called home from the post office and got the news that Dad's Uncle Doug from New Zealand was on his deathbed and if I didn't get out there right then I wouldn't see him. Doug was born on New Year's Day in 1920, he'd lied about his age to join the army at fourteen and was captured by the Japs at Hongkong on Christmas Day. He survived four years as a POW: slave labour in a copper mine, then shipped to Japan. He told me, when I visited him in the hospice, that he never liked killing people, but was so happy when they dropped the A-bombs and he knew it wouldn't be long: the Americans picked him up soon after, virtually blind and unable to walk from beriberi and pellagra.

Doug then went on to complete a twenty seven year career in the British army before settling in New Zealand; we all had a lot of respect for him. That was why I'd bought the one way ticket: he was the last of the old generation in our family and I'd missed all the other funerals in England the previous year. I hadn't even been aware that my relatives had died at the times they did – Intercontinental communications were not cheap and easy in the 80's and

90's before email and internet phones. We used aerogramme: that was my generation.

So Del didn't even know I wasn't coming straight back until he got a post card from New Zealand, that I didn't know for sure would even reach him. Nothing is worth what it was anymore, nothing is left to chance, now that everyone has a smart phone, sat-nav and facebook. There is no longer such a thing as a real adventure – a risky venture with an unknown outcome: travelling, for the vast majority of thrill seekers, is now a tailored pleasure opportunity, managed by computer geeks and you don't really have to know anything, anticipate anything or save your own life if it comes to it.

We drove on through the Northern Territories, into the early hours, and then parked up at another picnic site: in Australia it is better to sleep on a picnic bench than otherwise; I hate poisonous snakes and if you can get yourself off the ground, that has to be a good start. It was muggy and we were definitely in the tropics; it was a familiar sort of air, a cloudy sky, and I didn't even mind the mosquitoes: I figured that would mean the swarms of black flies wouldn't have followed us so far north.

When we got up in the morning we were in a different environment altogether. We were only five hundred kilometres from Darwin and the trees were bigger, the road wasn't straight anymore, it rained on and off and it was humid as hell. The Stuart Highway took us right into town and we found a backpackers' hostel only a block from the sea. It was reassuring to have the sea so close and knowing that the big empty continent was now behind me. It just so happened to be Good Friday and that meant that everything was closed.

I bought my onward flight to Kupang on the nearest Indonesian territory of West Timor, ready for the next leg of my journey. I wanted to island hop my way up to Singapore and I had one thousand US dollars to get me there and then on to Phnom Penh.

We took it easy all day, there were no beaches nearby and it was hot but the hostel had a pool and there were a lot of travellers hanging around, either just arrived, or ready to leave: it was a good place to sell a car if you needed to.

That evening I joined Oskar and Tolban in a small change Anzacs gambling game called 'Two-Up', involving tossing two coins up and betting they will both land heads or tails. We drank wine while we yelled and cursed our way through the game until it was time to go out to this new night club just opening that was aimed at back packers. It was advertised that they would be dishing out free food and drinks – that turned out too good to be entirely true. We did have a good time though and I went berserk, like I hadn't had a drink in months. The floor manager announced that there would be two jugs of beer for the first table where people got up and danced on it. I was up there before he finished his sentence and we got the beer. There were other tests and competitions to win drinks and prizes. I virtually crippled myself, trying to prove I could outride the local cowboys on the mechanical bull set up. I was thrown off so many times, but I wouldn't give up until I'd wrenched the muscles of both arms so badly I couldn't hardly pull myself back on the thing. Probably the most memorable thing was winning the Village People dance off, up on the stage – and I didn't even know the YMCA routine moves. I helped to break up a fight by wrestling some giant to the ground, then cart-wheeled across the dance floor, cracking the back of my head as I came up under a table. There was just one Aboriginal girl there and I tried to catch her eye, but it wasn't working, so I nicked all the unguarded drinks

I could spy around me, and rocked it out to *Nirvana* and oblivion. It's a wonder I found my way back to the hostel, which was quite some distance from the club, but I did it, with several rest stops along the way. I didn't drink again for at least a month.

I was useless the following day: I ached all over, I had a good selection of bruises, a terrible throat and I'd bitten my tongue quite badly. We all just lounged around the pool most of the day and I got into a discussion with a *Star Wars* fan who was lecturing a bunch of Yorkshire lads about alien contact that he claimed to have had. I mentioned I'd met a bloke called Peter Stammers who was from the star group Sirius; they all fell about laughing and moved on. I felt I should show a little empathy towards this young man with the oddly blue eyes, so I volunteered to hear him out. Once I told him I'd never seen *Star Wars*, he realised it wasn't going to go anywhere and wound it up.

The next day was the trip we planned to the Kakadu national park (*Crocodile Dundee* land) and we drove two or three hundred kilometres, right into it. First we drove past enormous termite mounds, then vast stretches of wetland to arrive at the Nourlangie Rock on higher ground. There were Aboriginal paintings on the rock faces in overhangs, some believed to be 20,000 years old, prehistoric hunting scenes and 'Dreamtime' mythology, but the most recent was a depiction of a rifle. The 'Lightning Dreaming Place', a sacred rocky escarpment that is never approached would have been visible from Nourlangi, but the atmosphere was fickle: a heavy black thunder cloud obscured the rock and we watched from the highpoint, as a huge low rainbow came towards us, then the rain engulfed our position and we ran for cover.

That night we camped out by a barbecue site and I chose

an old concrete base for myself while the Swedes slept in the car. I didn't put my net up, but just slept in my clothes with my hands and face covered. I forgot to tuck my jeans into my boots.

I woke up slapping my ankle, where a powerful stinging sensation was coming from. There's all sorts of deadly stuff out in the Australian bush: take your pick of the most lethal crawling creatures in the world. Instinct was to shake my legs and pat down my trousers, then logic took over and I opened up my maglite to do an inspection. I found a small yellow-green scorpion crouching down just beside me. I knew I had to get to a rangers' station quick, and I'd need to identify the creature, so, sitting up and trying to keep my legs still, I reached out with my knife and tried to skewer it. All I managed to do with the first stab was pin it down, just by the side of its abdomen. That made it mad, and it struggled furiously to break free, I had to release the blade to stab again, but missed, as it was running around in frenzy. I eventually got it and put it in a polythene bag, then hobbled to the car to wake the others.

They weren't too pleased, as it was gone midnight, but agreed that we had to get help. I couldn't push, so was in the diver's seat; I wouldn't use that leg at all, as I didn't want the blood moving around more than it had to. The track we were on was rough and they had to push quite hard to get up enough speed. Once it took, I gunned the engine without covering the brakes and the Swedes were running behind, shouting for me to stop. When it came to a halt and they caught up a hundred yards down the track they were even less impressed, but Torban drove with some urgency, while I was slumped in the passenger seat, drinking as much water as I could, in the hope it would thin down my body fluids a little. There were owls flying past the windscreen in panic as we powered on, I don't know how far, to the Cooinda Lodge ranger station.

Oskar and Torban helped me as I limped into the service building. I showed them my scorpion and the reaction was 'Oh, that fella's just like an angry ant'. Fine: I wasn't dying. Oskar went off back to the car in disgust and Torban and I went to the washroom block. I entered one of the cubicles and, as I assumed the position on the porcelain, I felt a tickle under my vest: 'Whoa!' this giant poisonous centipede was running for my armpit. I burst out of the cubicle yelling, with my trousers round my ankles and flinging off my vest. My clothes were in a pile in the middle of the floor and I was standing there naked, pointing at my clothes and yabbering on. Torban just stood there bemused, while I flicked at my clothing and a five inch black, writhing centipede scampered, with surprising speed, across the floor and up the wall.

So the scorpion just happened to have been on the scene and copped the blame. We didn't know how poisonous the centipede was, but as the bite had happened over an hour previously and I appeared to be fine, I didn't want to bother the rangers again that night. I just took a shower and then Torban and I sat out on the porch shelter, talking and watching wallabies hop around on the lawn. What a day!

We were booked on the early morning Yellow Water Cruise, and got loaded up with about a hundred other tourists hoping to see crocodiles etc. up one of the billabongs. A frog landed on my back and I lost it, yelling 'Get that off me! What is it?' That was quite embarrassing, for everyone involved, but quite funny really. We took it easy the rest of the day, just cruising around, looking for lizards and bird life. We made it back to the hostel that night and I was off to Timor, by plane, the next morning.

# CHAPTER 13: VIVA TIMOR-LESTE

Timor Island was a mountainous jungle plantation, fascinating and very basic. On arrival at the small airport in Kupang, I was stamped in and hustled into a taxi with two other travellers, heading for a place called 'Edan Homestay'. It was a death defying drive, fifteen kilometres, on windy roads. As soon as the car got going – Wham! The stereo came on full volume with double base; that would be par for the course on most of the small local transports (called Bemo) throughout the islands. The people had a mix of Malay and Melanesian blood and were sort of funny looking, in a pleasant enough way.

The home stay was out of town and beside a large and deep pool, fed by a spring and shaded by giant wide curtain trunk trees. People were swimming and washing in the pool, the kids smiled and the people were friendly.

At the guesthouse, things were overgrown with coconut and banana trees. I chose the least dank and dark looking of the filthy little cottages for 3000 Rupiah a night: less than two Aussi dollars. Apart from the mosquitoes getting through the holes in the net, there were bed bugs, a worm in my mandi (water tub they fill for you in your room, no shower) and a mouse that ate my soap, and I think lives in the spare mattress.

The night bus to Dili in East Timor took twelve hours, and we got a puncture on the way. There was no spare, but they swapped the duel wheels around somehow, leaving just

one on each side. They had no jack either and the job was done by balancing rocks up under the axel.

Dili was a strange city, for a multitude of reasons: the first thing to do was to change money as I was down to my last 5000R; it took one hour to do this in the bank. This was obviously normal, as a TV was set up in the building to keep people occupied while they waited. I got to watch a whole episode of *The Dukes of Hazard* which was playing. I noticed there were quite a few Indonesian soldiers on the street, East Timor, or Timor-Leste as the locals called it, was still under occupation by the Indonesian army, who had a tight hold on it.

I tried, for the second day running, to buy a boat ticket to Larantuka on Flores Island, but no luck in finding the office open, so I got to the mini-bus station at a dirty market suburb called Becora just in time to board the bus to Los Palos, near the North East tip of the island. There were several stops at police checkpoints, where everyone was herded off the bus by police with long bamboo sticks in their hands. I asked one what the sticks were for and he smiled and said 'No use'. In Los Palos I was dropped off at a simple guesthouse they call a losmen. The owner could only speak Portuguese with me, so I managed to remember a bit from my South American adventures. He told me he had recently suffered with malaria. Great, I thought, as I had been bitten two or three times, while sitting talking with him. I had realised that everywhere I went in East Timor, I was getting approached and befriended by either Indonesian spies, or Timorese patriots: some could have been in either camp but testing me out to see if I had any allegiances. They all wanted to know who I had met and if I had friends in the country. I watched a volleyball match played by Indonesian police women, they were quite good. Then I got met by a plain clothes police officer from Lombok, who insisted on walking me to the police station to register where I was staying. The cops inside were all playing cards, and I asked a few questions, they had five hundred officers stationed in tiny Los Palos alone, but the boss man assured me there was no trouble in East Timor anymore. I told them we had just one officer stationed in my own village to manage three thousand people, and that on the road up to this town, we'd passed a mini-bus by the side of the road, with all the windows shattered and the bodywork scarred by rocks and bullets. He wanted to know about Princess Di, and also did we have free sex in England?

I'd checked the guest list back at the losmen when I booked in. Only two Westerners had signed in, and that was a month and a half ago. I love coming to these edge of the world places that tourists bypass, it's not convenient or cheap (for what you get) but you do get a taste of the real world.

Since Christmas time I had been suffering from a gut problem that I was pretty sure was down to amoebas in the Phnom Penh water. I'd had to pay a shocking amount to see a doctor in New Zealand, just to get the prescription that allowed me to buy one dose worth of Fasigyn. That cleared me for a week or more, then I felt the tell-tale signs re-emerging and had to spend out on a second visit. That wasn't the end of the story as once I got to Australia I knew I had company again. I did sort that protozoan out in the end, after I got to Indonesia and could get metronidazole without a prescription. I decided to double dose, to be sure this time, and then waited six days and double dosed again. That cured it.

I had to be up and out by five am to catch the bemo to the furthest point, Tutuala. It was a long bumpy track, just dirt in places and I had to register my passport twice at polisi check point offices.

The only accommodation was a fine looking colonial hotel, perched at the end of the world, five hundred metres above the sea, but no way down to it through the thick, tangled jungle. It was a perfect location for a grand villa and couldn't have been a more dramatic site, to mark the beginning of one of the most exotic island chains in the world. Fifteen minutes later I was less pleased: the old man in charge showed me around and there were just four large rooms with multiple beds to take my pick of. There were two bathrooms, with dust and dirt, water on the floor but no running water, and there was only one mandi; it had a foot of stagnant water in it. None of the beds had clean sheets and the man was jesting at 20,000R: I got him down to 10,000 by speaking Portuguese and giving him a postcard of London.

There was no warung (eating house) and the only shop in the village had no drinking water; so I bought three cans of warm Sunkist and made do with a tin of sardines. I managed to beg some boiled water from a house nearby, before I set off on the eight kilometre walk to the East Beach. A kilometre or so along the trail, I overtook a woman with two young children, and when she noticed me, she pulled her kids right over to one side of the track, staring in alarm at me: it was sort of funny. Eventually I got to the beach, after taking a wrong fork of the trail, which left me scrambling over rocks and through secondary jungle, until I emerged from the trees on a virgin paradise: white sand, palm and pandanus trees, and an uninhabited coral island offshore. I didn't bother with the trunks when I went for my swim; the water was calm, clean and warm. I walked round the rocky undercut to the south and came across several small outrigger canoes and there were three fishermen with eight foot long home made spear-guns. They eyed me suspiciously; the tall one in a wide brimmed hat only had one good eye. Then I greeted them in Portuguese and they suddenly became easier. Portuguese was the colonial language of Timor-Leste and has been suppressed by the Indonesian occupation. When you spoke it there, people knew where your sympathies lay.

I found the main path back up to Tutuala, it had grave sites at some intervals and they were marked by cement tiers with a cross and a beer bottle; many had buffalo skulls with crucifixes mounted on them. The washing spring was just before the village, over a bridge at the top of the trail. I saw the same woman with her two kids there, and she was over her initial shock at seeing a European man. There was a small group of them and they were very amused by me washing my clothes at their spring. More and more kept arriving and I was able to swap my last can of Sunkist for a fresh coconut, several knives and machetes were offered for me to open it with. I did have some biscuits and offered them out, but no one would take them at first, then this one little girl with wild hair, sort of snatched the small packet like a monkey might. Everyone laughed as she kept the packet close by her side, very funny it was.

Three boys escorted me back up to the villa and Armando, the losmen keeper, invited me into his parlour for coffee. His father had been in the Portuguese army in Mozambique and his mother was a native Timorean. He was despondent about the situation, he ran the losmen for the officials but his heart wasn't in it; he still carried a twenty Escudos note in his wallet, old and torn, it hadn't been currency in Timor for twenty years. The sun set beyond the jungle shoreline, lending the trees a dark red glow above the black water.

It had rained in the night and I got transport half way back to Dili, stopping off at the town of Baucau. The Hotel Flamboyan was the only place in town; a big government run flat-roofed building, as I remember it, on a high rise. I've read since then that this building was used by the Indonesian army as a torture centre; I didn't know that then. On a walk around the town, I bumped into a couple of foreign journalists who had to travel around with Indonesian escorts. The chaperones were shadowing them and didn't like that their charges had stopped to speak with an independent traveller; we swapped some info and split before the goons approached. Baucau was an interesting place, the second largest city in Timor-Leste: built across rock fissures on the side of a bit of a plateau from where you could view the sea, about five kilometres away. I followed a small lane going uphill and it led me past the fourteen stages of the cross. At the top of the rock, three or four locals were building a new church.

That night, I was woken by shouting, and I went to my balcony window to see. It was a drunken Brazilian standing out on his balcony, one floor up from me, bellowing out anti-establishment revolutionary slogans. He had a good collection of international heroic statements, in French, Spanish, Portuguese and English. He was Castro, Haile Selassie, General Francisco Franco and Napoleon Bonaparte. It was brilliant, a protest against the regime, 'Viva Timor libra', 'Viva independencia de Timor total' 'Viva FRETILIN'; I thought he would be arrested for sure, but nothing happened, other people came out onto their balconies, and half the town must have heard it, as it went on for twenty minutes or more and carried across the silent town below. FRETILIN stands for Frente Revolucionaria de Timor-Leste Independente: that's the Cuban style rebels up in the mountains. If a Timorese was shouting that stuff from his house in town, then the regime would have been round and he would disappear.

I was lucky to walk down the steps of the hotel in the morning and almost immediately flag down the bus from Los Palos to take me to Dili. The bus was stopped by polisi on the way, everyone was out and they were checking ID cards. They didn't ask to see my passport but the friendly Javanese man, who was obviously connected, made a point of checking out my purpose. I'd been warned to be careful in handling conversations with these agents of the state and I made a point of asking more questions than he could of me 'til the bus was ready to continue.

At the overpriced guest huts in Dili, I met a frustrated Norwegian called Per Olav, who was having trouble with taxis and accommodation. He was okay, and we walked to the Pelni shipping office again: my fourth attempt to buy passage to the next island. They wouldn't sell tickets in the afternoon, so we just walked along to the dirty grey beach, where the youths of Dili played football and watched a game. Very quickly we became the centre of attention, with dozens of young men posing for photos, showing victory signs and pledging their lives to 'Timor-Leste' once the uprising came, and they said it would be soon. They asked us to take the message out to the world, as they said any letters they might send out would be intercepted by the authorities, who would then come knocking. We took a couple of letters to post for them, once off the island and in another country, not from Indonesia. Per and I walked the four kilometres to Areia Branca, the white beach with the Jesus statue on the promontory, like a miniature of the Christ the Redeemer at Rio de Janeiro.

That evening, Per and I went out to the Hawaiian Bakery

for coffee and cake. Two youths, who had been shadowing us half the day, found us and offered to guide us to the mountains in the Baucau area to find the FRETILIN commander, Konis Santana. Santana was their Che Guevara and of course it would be incredible to have gone up there: but to make that arrangement in a public eatery, with strangers we couldn't understand, at night! It was close, but we declined and agreed to speak with them further during daylight hours, when we could see who was listening in.

The main man was called Antonio Branco Soares and we couldn't understand a word he said at first. We asked if it was English, and it was, but he had taught himself from books, so he knew a lot but couldn't pronounce anything; it was a ridiculously confusing conversation and we had to give him a pen and paper to write his questions down on.

The following day, we decided to pay a visit to the residence of the Nobel Peace Prize laureate, the Bishop Belo – one lad we met at the football game lived at the compound, so we got an introduction. If we were considering going to meet the guerrilla leader – if – then we wanted advice from this highly respected man, and we were pretty sure there would be no spies eavesdropping in the secure compound. We were a couple of fools who didn't really know enough about the country and the situation: but Bishop Belo did, and if he said no, we wouldn't go.

He met us on the veranda briefly; I wrote at the time that he was a short man, with a hard face and some scarring to one temple. He shook our hands firmly, without smiling, and the thing I noticed immediately was the huge gold ring on the third finger of his right hand. Well that was as far as it went and we were told to make an appointment with his secretary at the post office, but he wouldn't be able to see anybody until half way into the next week and it was only Saturday. We weren't journalists on a retainer, we were travellers on a budget, things happened if the bricks slotted into place at the right times, if they didn't you moved on before your money ran out; so that's what I did.

I learned that the Pelni ship Tatamailau sailed for Larantuka at 11am and it was already ten o'clock gone. If I caught this ship I would cut out the Solor and Alor islands, save time and money and get on with the journey. So I stuffed things into my bags, got a taksi to the port and boarded the ship. They wouldn't sell me a ticket on board, so I ran down the gangway with thirty five minutes to spare. One helpful local took one of my bags for me and we ran through the crowded port to find a taksi. I got to the Pelni office (the fifth attempt), bought a ticket and got back to the harbour with twenty five minutes to go. As I walked towards the ship, people started to shout and I saw the gangway rising. I was running again, with a full rucksack and two other bags, shouting 'Hey! Hey! Hey!' and the people shouted too. The gangway disappeared on a fork-lift truck but they started to lower some narrow sidesteps for me. It was great timing, the people were whooping and cheering as I started to climb and I gave them a 'Viva Timor-Leste' once I reckoned I was safe.

I was sorry not to meet up with some of the footballers again, Manuel and Amali; I often wonder what happened to them in 1999, when the state killing machine was unleashed just before Indonesia left East Timor and they finally did get their independence. I know Antonio Branco Soares made it through, working for the UN once they did arrive. Nino Konis Santana had died, during an ambush, I read, the year before. If I hadn't been tied up with Cambodia and everything going on there, I do think I would have been back in 'Loro Sae' (the native Tetum name for the island, which means the land of the rising sun), to see it all for myself.

I was too late to get a mattress space on board Tatamailau, but it didn't matter. She sounded her horn and pulled away just before eleven that morning and I stood on the side looking at the port, the lighthouse and the fine looking church, less gaudy than most catholic structures, kinder looking.

# CHAPTER 14: SINGAPORE SLING

The journey north through the Indonesian archipelago is best described in my original words taken from a journal I wrote at the time. Some parts have been condensed, simplified or omitted altogether to enable the narrative to flow and to retain the spirit of the telling.

**Saturday, 20th April 1996    NUSA TENGGARA**
'I looked out at the path the ship had left, a load of rubbish had just been dumped and I watched it drift in the wake. Then there were fins and bodies splashing amongst it, large sharks, a pack of twenty I would say. But the ship travels fast and it was soon lost in the distance. I went to the side a bit later to look on the rugged mountains of Pulau Alor, as we cruised along its northern coast. All of a sudden, there she blew! It was a Sperm Whale, quite close off the port beam: then there were more, further out, blowing and diving. It was really a great sight, totally unexpected: five, six, maybe seven of them. I know the villagers from some of these islands, still hunt them in small boats, with hand held harpoons.

There were basic rice meals served on board, which was a good thing, as I'd had no time to bring food with me: but by sundown I was getting fed up with being interrupted by other passengers, trying to interact with me when they can see I'm reading a book; it's hard travelling alone in a contained public space, I try to hold onto my patience and not appear rude, but I just want to shut it all out. I've been doing all this for seven years almost, because, I suppose, I didn't know what else to do. Well now I have plans and ideas, I don't feel like I really need it all now. I'm not thinking much about the road ahead, I just want to get to the other side, what I see on the way is what I see. The best experiences to have are always unplanned and unexpected.

### Sunday, 21st April          FLORES

I was off the boat and on a bus bound for Maumere by 12.00 midnight. It was full of the most nauseating Indonesians I've met so far: rude, self pleasing discourteous people coughing and sneezing; men sporting effeminate postures and women's finger nails, trying to chat me up, or just calling 'Hello Mister' and giggling. The bus arrived in Maumere about four am and I got a hotel room, then I slept for half the day.

### Monday, 22nd April

I got on the bus to Moni at eight am, it set off straight away but just went round and round the town, picking people up on the way and at eight forty I was back at the bus station! The road to Moni (three hours plus) was so steep and windy that I felt a bit sick myself; the locals were vomiting into plastic bags the whole way. Moni is a collection of villages rather than a town, it is the stop over for visiting the multi coloured crater lakes of Kelimutu; it is also a transport hub for the busses running the length of Flores Island and everyone stops there.

### Wednesday, 24th April

I caught the bus (six hours) to Bajawa, really great scenery, tremendous gorges and numerous volcanoes to look at on the way. I didn't enjoy the ride though, as I was squashed up on the back seat with two mothers and their little girls. Both kids and one of the mothers were sick, copiously, into plastic bags right beside me; one poor little girl had it all down her, she didn't seem to mind. It was an oddly amusing experience seeing mother and daughter, both throwing up; one out of the open door and the other into a giant clear polythene bag that had been passed around and was pretty full. We had a very close call, with a truck coming round the bend towards us and we were on his side of the road. Both trucks swerved and I braced myself for the impact to crush my legs when the seats folded.

### Thursday, 25th April

The next nine hour bus journey completed the seven hundred kilometre Trans Flores road. The island itself is only 375 kms in length! Actually I enjoyed the final part of the journey, as I decided to sit on the roof for the winding, twisting descent to Labuan Bajo. It felt like a roller coaster ride on horseback. I'd been inside to start with, and admiring the volcano Gunung Inerie, which dominated the view. Then people started boffing up all over the show, with calls for "plastic, plastic!" There were two boys in the seat in front of me, the smallest one was being sick down his front at regular intervals and then his older brother yakked all over the poor kid's lap and his legs. I'd never seen someone so covered in chunder before in my life. When that family got off at their stop, I could see the seat and floor was covered in it.

Labuan Bajo has a romantic natural harbour setting, full of outrigger boats, you can't see the open sea for the many small islands scattered out there, it was a great sunset.

## Saturday, 27th April      The boat to Lombok

There were twelve of us tourists taking the cruise, and five crew on board the thirty foot fishing boat. I wasn't really doing this five day cruise for pleasure, but it was convenient, stopping at several places I wanted to see and saving me the land journey across Sumbawa. We stopped off for some snorkelling at Bidadari Island then on to Rinca, where we saw our first Komodo dragons, at a distance.

## Sunday, 28th April      Komodo Island

We came ashore in the dugout and immediately came upon the first dragon. It was much bigger than the ones from yesterday, and had been lounging around beside the bridge we crossed. It was big enough to be a real danger if it wanted to move and it had no fear of us. We had a guide come ashore with us from our boat who warned us that they get fed once a week, but roam free anywhere on the island and can run down prey like wild pigs and buffalos. He said that at least three tourists, who'd wandered off alone on the islands, had been eaten by the lizards over the last few years. This one was up to three metres long and was showing an interest in us. It came out of the dry stream bed into the clearing and sat up, smelling the air with its forked tongue for our scent, we never saw the teeth but it had long sharp talons that looked lethal. I edged towards it to get a good picture and the guide went crazy.

We struggled to get the engine going, and then motored off to Gili Laba, a nearby uninhabited island; they were dry scrubby islands, not real jungle, with shallow water, fish and coral. That evening some people complained of paraffin oil in the pineapple slices, then Dean, a rigger from Cairn, gave a didgeridoo demonstration, it sounded great as I'd never heard one played properly before, the sounds were raw and hypnotic.

We weighed anchor after sunset and motored, with our jib set (the only sail the boat possessed) all night. As night came on, the southern stars came out and we seemed to be following Venus as she came down to meet the waves, I woke around eleven, there was a bit of a swell and the occasional splash of spray. I played my harmonica softly as we sailed towards the setting moon.

### Monday, 29th April

We sailed on all day, stopping around noon to visit a beach on the northern coast of Sumbawa, where there was a fresh water source and we could wash the salt out of our hair. When it was time to leave, the engine started but there was no transmission. That took a while to sort out in the engine room, and three or four of us dived to observe the propeller. We did get underway and made it to Satonda Island, where we anchored for the night. We saw two fish eagles and then hundreds of flying foxes took to the sky after sunset.

### Tuesday, 30th April

Next stop was Moyo Island: getting closer to Lombok. There was fresh water there too, so I washed the salt from my hair, body and clothes. Standing on the beach I saw a fin splash the water surface and two of the crew dived in to catch it. It was a big, big fish with a beautiful blue sheen to its skin, and it was dying. The crew were happy and would barbecue it later this evening. We weren't so sure about eating a sick and dying fish, until we found another a few miles further on and the crew explained that people used dynamite around these islands and that was probably why they died. We went on round to the west coast of the island and that's where we came ashore to make the fire.

The fish was cooked, and we all ate it, somehow one of the chickens we were carrying got free from the wheelhouse roof and flew out towards the land. The poor thing landed in the water and bobbed around a bit before striking out for the shore. It must have been paddling furiously as it was making good headway; I'd never seen a chicken swim before. We were all cheering it on from the boat, but the crew were launching the canoe; the chicken saw this and kept going for freedom. When they caught it up, the first thing it did was jump straight back into the sea.

That night I watched the sunset and the silhouette of the Rinjani volcano on Lombok, it was a triangular cone, split at the top like a V shape: 3700 metres plus and I was planning to climb it.

### Wednesday, 1st May
I woke up at two am as the engine fired up and the boat steered ever west, into the setting moon. It was a bit of a rough night as the boat lurched to and fro, with the spray coming over heavier and heavier. We made one last stop for lunch, off a tiny island where we did a last snorkel dive, there was not much coral, just banks of black sea urchins, and they had tiny blue coral fish in amongst their spines. The last meal at sea was just rice and noodles, and some chicken knuckle bones: no vegetables and two of the sauces had run out. There was paraffin in the pineapple for the third time and the drinking water had run out.

I beat Richard at chess, finally, after losing to him twice every day. It felt good, because he didn't like it. He had shaken people's hands patronisingly at the end of all the games he'd won throughout the trip to force an admission of defeat: when it came to his turn and he knew he couldn't win, he just gave in his king. I didn't really get on with half of the other passengers, and couldn't wait to get ashore and move on. For the last hour or so I just stood on the deck, looking out at Lombok and its massive volcano, I knew that with every splash and roll of the boat, I was coming closer to journey's end.'

\*\*\*

The best thing I did on this whole trip was to climb Gunung Rinjani. I was up there for four days and three nights, and it was the highest mountain I had ever climbed before: 3726 metres, virtually from sea level. It was a two day hike, up and over the main rim and into the four mile wide crater of the active volcano. It was raining some of the way during the first day, going through the forest in the cloud band; but that was left behind as the vegetation petered out and the going got tough.

The view from the crater ridge was one I'll never forget; a huge, wide lozenge of water, in different hues of blue, with a barren, moonlike, grey-black extrusion of smoking lava field at the near side; its baby cinder-cone volcano looking so fine, like a chocolate truffle. It was a great place to watch the sunset, and almost straight after it had gone, the full moon rose from the north side, it was a slightly orange colour, reflected from the sunset sky. There was a series of hot springs running down into the lake, that changed the colour of the water from cobalt blue to a milky turquoise colour and I stayed one night down by the springs.

The following afternoon, I hiked up to the crater rim the other side of the springs. I made my camp up on this eastern shoulder of the ridge that led up to the highest peak and I was ready for the final push. Other people started arriving in the evening, mostly Indonesian students, I would guess.

The final climb started at three in the morning and took me just under three hours to get to the top. It was so hard with my rucksack on, trudging in the dark, up a path of loose volcanic grit. I managed to pace myself to the level of oxygen I was getting at that altitude: overtaking, one by one, the people who had started ahead of me. It was so steep and my feet slid down one step for every two I took in the ash and cinder. I got there, arriving at the summit in time to witness all the stages of dawn from a mountain top: that first grey-blue tinge, where you become aware of the horizon. One by one, the stars fade out and that dark red glow appears, then you get a wider band of pink and purple. Finally yellow and blue, and then it's there, that beam of light you've been longing for, and you feel the rays of the sun despite the freezing wind. Then you know it has all been worth it.

It was good; Lombok Island is basically a huge volcano, rearing up out of the sea, and from the top, before the cloud moved in, it was possible to see most of the coastline, as well as other islands I'd been to and those which I had not yet seen.

It didn't stop being hard work on the way down either; I was carrying everything I owned and I took the short cut, straight down the eastern slope, once I'd got back to the shoulder and made some breakfast. It was all loose surface, and vast: streaked with dry rain gullies and ravines. I got down by halfway though the afternoon and came across a mountain trekking lodge, where I was able to swap my sleeping bag and rain jacket for a night's accommodation, evening meal and breakfast: this still left me 5000R for the bemo back to my starting point at Senaru. I left my ruined boots there for a local guide to make something of and suffered the nauseating trip south to the port town of Lembar: I get car-sick sometimes, but here it's like the national sport of Nusa Tenggara – never sit near children in a bemo.

I met an English girl called Jo in the taksi to the ferry and sold her my mask and snorkel (money was getting tight and I wasn't going to need them in Cambodia, any more than I would my sleeping bag). We got on okay and travelled together to Ubud in Bali where I rested up a few days. Ubud is billed as the cultural centre of the island, and the first Hindu place I'd visited. It was there that I came across that crazy Brazilian, Ricardo, from the Hotel Flamboyan. I recognized him immediately and walked up to his café table and said 'Je suis Napoleon Bonaparte'. We instantly hit it off, I don't normally fit in with new people, but that man had earned my respect.

Really, the adventure came to an end as I got the bemo full of back packers to Kuta Beach. It was the most awful tourist hole I'd ever been to; the beach was full of massage women, T-shirt girls, surf board hire stalls and any number of mobile vendors, selling drinks, lighters, crap jewellery etc. The beach was clogged with Australians on holiday; fat topless lobsters, and even the local touts had copied their accents: 'Hey mate, you want a bong', 'massage', 'tattoo', 'pedicure', 'marijuana', 'sarong', 'Billabong T-shirt', 'You buy short'. I hated it and rented a motorbike to get me out to a cliff top temple where a monkey snatched my sunglasses.

The rest of the trip, through Java and on to Singapore, was a holiday. I can't say it was really travelling; it was mainly good roads, tourist class long distance busses and food you wanted to eat. Don't get me wrong, Java was a remarkable place, full of nature and culture: I visited the famous Mt

Bromo (full of Jap tourists and cloudy), Borobudor and Prambanan temples (impressive, but a bit sterile), the best part, certainly, was getting chatted up by dozens of student girls in hijabs. Nothing was particularly difficult anymore and apart from a short break in Yogyakarta, where I bought some decent clothes and gave up my decaying rucksack for a set of stylish leather suitcases (I wanted to arrive in Phnom Penh in style), it was not that memorable either. This is what I wrote about Jakarta:

**Wednesday, 22nd May**
'The train was better than I thought it would be, but still bloody hot and uncomfortable. I could only get any reasonable sleep on the floor in the aisle, as I saw other people doing. This was okay except for the frequent stops when the vendors all file through. The train arrived at 3.15 am and when I got out to the tuk tuk corner and started haggling for a price to Jalan Jaksa, I realised I had either left one plastic carrier bag on the train, or some bastard had just lifted it from beside my feet as I bargained. It had my Lonely Planet guide to South East Asia, my shampoo and toothbrushes and paste, my spare malaria pills, some food and teabags, my gum shield from Thai Boxing and the copy of Time magazine I only bought last night, before I got on the train.

My first impressions of Jakarta are: it's a big bustling polluted Asian mega-city, over-priced but not unattractive. I don't much like staying here at Jalan Jaksa, it's expensive, the hostel staff are like Chinese zombies, there are Arabs staying here, and Africans in the cafes: It's suspicious, no doubt about it; they don't travel and they don't appear to work, packing together, ghetto style, in every capital city in Asia: why?

On a short walk around the back alleys I noticed raw sewage trickling from pipes in the bottom of the walls and flowing along the open drains either side of the path; so much for the modern façade.'

I did visit the old town called Kota, that was Dutch Batavia and the working port of Sunda Kelapa that was full of the traditional Makasa sailing schooners. They were loading and off-loading goods, some were having their wooden hulls repainted. There were fortified spice houses, the old Dutch watchtower and some rusted canons: the remnants of a great trading empire; crumbling walls holding back the refuse that was rotting in the stagnant channel below. There were market stalls and the narrow slum streets across the water. The grey open sewers and small canals, crossed by rickety wooden planks, were the veins of daily life, with small boats bringing goods inland from the port with the tide which also took the sewage back out with it.

I got to witness a freak show in the street, amongst the rubble and filth; a group of amateur entertainers were playing drums and glockenspiels, as a fire eater, with sensitive lips, cracked a whip over the body of another member of the troupe, who was trussed up like a chicken. They had two vagabond boys, rolling around in the dirt, dancing and gurning in cloth hoods and masks; they seemed to be entranced. The one with the harelip was ducking for bits of vegetable in a bucket of dirty water and then he ate a light bulb and washed it down with some of that water. The whole thing was grotesque.

I met a bunch of university students on the train back to Jalan Jaksa who fired off the usual questions at me. They were okay really and walked me back to my block, where we sat in a café and drank lemon juice. The one girl in the bunch, Santi, who I didn't like much at first (she was a bit too quick and clever, with her baseball cap and American dialect), gave me her phone number as they left. I called her and we met up the next morning. We went around together the whole day and it was nice, apart from the arguments about East Timor and Saddam Hussein. We ate at an international café round the corner from my hostel and I ordered Indonesian, while she ordered Western food; we were both disappointed. I picked up my cases then and caught the bus to the airport for my evening flight to Singapore, then slept in one of the lounges, before getting myself downtown to find another hostel for my couple of nights' stay in the city.

I left Singapore's Changi Airport on the morning of the 28th May, having spent my last day's budget on a Singapore sling at the long bar in Raffles Hotel. I hadn't ever intended forking out nine quid for a pink gin on my travels, not when I wasn't paying that for a bed. But the mood took me, as I chatted with a Canadian back-packer who'd also come to view the famous slab of timber. We laughed when the waiter asked if we wanted to order another.

# PART THREE
# BREAK-BONE FEVER

# CHAPTER 15: YELLOW RIVER

I was on the Royal Air Cambodge (the former national carrier of Cambodia) 737-400 plane named 'Angkor Wat', bound for an awful and incredible country, whose people I both loved and hated. I flew across the sea to the east of the Malay Peninsular. The sky turned dark and turbulence hit, rocking the plane, I didn't worry, I knew I was getting home. An hour or more later we came clear and I looked down on the coast-line of Cambodia. It felt good to see it, a strange and primeval land – green forest, rocky hills, temples, dirt roads and water. Soon I was looking down on the rice bowl plain and it looked a stagnant yellow; as the sun caught each plot, I could see it was flooded. The in-flight radio was playing 'Yellow River' which caught the feeling just right.

I felt a tightening inside me as the plane touched down. I stepped out onto the concrete apron, into that familiar engulfing heat and walked past three or four Khmer women in their traditional finery, waiting in the heat to greet some VIP, but it wasn't me. I was going back to what I knew, but I was going to make a success of it this time.

I had wanted to arrive in Phnom Penh in style, even if I had only $100 US, a $20 traveller's cheque, £30 cash and $50 Singapore. It would be a start, and I would pick up work as soon as I could. I had ditched the back-pack and was carrying a set of real leather suitcases I'd bought in

Yogyakarta, plus I was wearing all new city clothes I'd got from a department store.

I found Del – he was no longer working at the same school, or staying at the same place. One of the moto-dops, Tree, I think, took me over to the new place he was renting (for more than he could afford). The taxi guys had told me, 'Del not same as before, very *skoam* (thin).' And they weren't joking either; I was shocked when the door opened and his sunken eyes squinted out, I actually did think he might be dying. He had been ill, of course, and was living on sweets, condensed milk and 7up. He had broken a bone in his foot from a moped crash, and one in his hand from punching the sofa. After six months, left to his own devices, he had only $20 in his bank and just enough in his pocket to last him out the week.

One of my last diary entries for the whole Asian adventure sets the tone with some despondency:

**Friday, 31ˢᵗ May 1996**

'I've just arrived in the place I've been trying to get to for four months, and by midday today I've become totally disillusioned with my purpose for being here. The political situation is rotten; the social and moral ideals popularly practiced and accepted are just pure basic barbarism. The Khmer people are like a savage and primitive tribe, thrown in confusion into the C20ᵗʰ. The security situation apparently is becoming critical and foreigners are increasingly being targeted for hold-ups; mostly the robbers are spoilt rich kids, the teenage sons of high ranking police and military. They carry guns to school and ride Suzuki Crystals. Hun Sen goons have executed several Khmer journalists who had written critically about the government. The whole lot of them are still doing deals with Malaysia, the Thai military and the Khmer Rouge to cooperate in the illegal logging of all of Cambodia's forests. Elections in 98? The outlook is bleak, if the constitution lasts that long. All the hopes and expectations that came with the UNTAC mission are worthless; good people risked their lives, and some of them died to bring "free and fair" elections and democracy to this land, but mostly bad people abused, benefitted and exploited it all. Now corruption here is worse than in 1970.'

Within two days of arriving in the country I had a part-time teaching job and within two months we were both working full time at one of the best private schools in the country. I was courting a lovely lady called Sithikesravottey and a fortune teller had told Del to watch out for V.D. and a man who was going to shoot him in the head.

The rest of that year was remarkable for many reasons and they are all covered in a book I am still working on called Kingdom of the Monkey. We will leave it there for now, but suffice it to say, Del and I both made it out of that place and the river of life went on.

*So long boy you can take my place, got my papers I've got my pay*
*So pack my bags and I'll be on my way to yellow river*
*Put my guns down the war is won*
*Fill my glass high the time has come*
*I'm going back to the place that I love yellow river*
*Yellow river, yellow river is in my mind and in my eyes*
*Yellow river, yellow river is in my blood, it's the place I love*
*Got no time for explanations, got no time to lose*
*Tomorrow night you'll find me*
*Sleeping underneath the moon at yellow river*
*Cannon fire lingers in my mind, I'm so glad that I'm still alive*
*And I've been gone for such a long time from yellow river*

*I remember the nights were cool I can still see the water pool*
*And I remember the girl that I knew from yellow river*
*Yellow river, yellow river is in my mind and in my eyes*
*Yellow river, yellow river is in my blood, it's the place I love*

Written by Jeff Christie in 1970

# CHAPTER 16: BLUE LIGHTS AND BROKEN DREAMS

In August 1997 I was back in my caravan field, on the farm, with my new wife. We had skipped the country after the battles during a military takeover the month before.

I was having a hard time trying to adjust and settle down. I know it must have been so much harder for Vottey, and I wasn't the best at showing understanding. I had a need to be away on my own, as often as I could justify and I'm not sorry for that. I needed excitement and a sense of purpose. There was no way I was ready for a family life, it wouldn't have been right or fair on anyone.

After the Millennium, which wasn't what it was cracked up to be, a turn of events persuaded me to make some changes. I had scraped out a living, trying out various past time employments and self generated business ventures. Although it was sustainable, none of my efforts were going to buy us a home of our own. I had answered a local newspaper ad for an opportunity to train as a regional sales executive for a company pushing protective wall coatings. I'd had a couple of suits, made up in Bangkok before we'd left, but I needed the right car.

The White Charger still ran, but was never going back on the road. I still had Grandad's little Mini van, but it was starting to suffer; the brakes, petrol pump, carb' and alternator all had age problems. The poor thing had never been right really, after I'd driven it through a local flood and it actually floated. The Mini was not up to the job of commuting up to London anyway, so Dad took me off for a tour of the second hand car yards in the area. The first one we went to turned out to be run by Sam Lillywhite, an old school friend of mine. Sam managed to sell me a BMW320i, a two door saloon, with sunroof, in silver. It was another C reg. but rather nice, and the flashiest car I had ever driven. It was also my most expensive car, at eighteen hundred pounds.

The fact that I jacked in the training course, after the first week, didn't matter: I had a proper car that made me feel like I was making it in life. Although no longer living in a caravan in a field, I certainly wasn't 'making it'. I did love roaring it along the sea front at Hythe, early in the morning, with the promenade and sea wall on one side, the Military Canal on the other, it's shapely bonnet gleaming in the watery sunlight.

That was one of the last regular cars made that was modelled, to some extent, on the aestheticism of the human form. This one was a little androgynous, I thought, but it was the closest any of my cars had got to representing any kind of sex appeal. Most cars, post Millennium, seem to be designed to look like the average overweight forty year old on their way to the swimming pool – where they will probably do a couple of lengths, then wallow around at the edge, before getting out and sitting at the café with a slimmer's coffee in a takeaway cup.

Of course, I didn't look after that car properly, and when the rad' showed signs of not being able to keep the temperature regulated, I would simply switch the fan on and pop the bonnet catch whilst on the move. It had a weird mechanism, where the whole bonnet would catch the air over a certain speed, lifting it parallel to the engine bay, three inches up, and hold itself there, straight and level. The fresh air was forced over the top of the engine and straight out at the windscreen end. This worked fine at moderate speeds, but getting stuck in a three hour traffic jam, whilst trying to cross central London, killed it off. The head gasket was finished, and the automatic viscous fan mechanism no longer worked. The power steering and brakes were also pretty much useless by the time I parked her up in the caravan field in early 2002.

By this time I had a proper job and a mortgage on a nice little house in Sellindge, built on the old Ken Cork mowers site, right next door to Kestrels. Rodger had sold up and so it was no longer a communal bachelor pad-cum-party house. A letter from Kent County Constabulary, promising meaningful employment had got me the buying power we needed instantly, before I'd even done a day's work at it. Then I found that I was stuck in a job I quickly realised that I hated, more than any job I'd ever had.

The funny thing was, they put all us recruits through a basic driving course and evaluated our abilities to drive a police car. Most of the girlies couldn't reverse for toffee, but they all passed with big smiles. I on the other hand, failed three basic assessments and one standard assessment. One instructor did state that I had the best natural ability when it came to the skid pan section, *of any novice he had ever taught*. They just didn't like my style; still, it wasn't me driving two years later, when our Peugeot 306 jack-knifed at 80 mph one frosty night on the Smarden Bell road, slamming it into a tree at a location the local teams called 'the Screaming Woods'.

The hit came on my front wing and the impact forced the wheel up into the passenger foot-well, striking my left foot and chipping a piece of bone from my heel. The airbags went off, but I hadn't seen it happen; so, believing that the powder filling the car was smoke, I started to panic when my door wouldn't open. We had bounced right back out into the middle of the road and I just rolled myself head first out of the smashed side window, onto the road and ran for the safety of the trees. Once I knew I'd made it, I realised that I couldn't stand and sunk to the ground, while our racing driver, Si Ozzy, started to panic too. He was more worried about his career than my foot, I think, as the first thing he did was pull out my fluorescent motorway jacket and give it to the prisoner we had been transporting in the back. Never mind me sitting on the cold earth.

Simon reported the crash, to our section Sergeant, over the radio, but didn't confirm that we needed an ambulance, not for half an hour anyway. Once the cones were set out, I did say I was cold, so Si and the prisoner helped me to get laid out across the back seat of the wrecked panda car. Simon was buzzing around, trying to remember his training. He went to the boot to rummage for the POLICE ACCIDENT signs and picked up my heavy PSU (Police Support Unit) bag containing all my riot gear. The dick-head grabbed it out and chucked it across the back seat space in the car: right onto my outstretched legs, I couldn't believe it!

Actually, Simon was a decent bloke, just young and over enthusiastic. I later refused to let the PSD (Professional Standards Department) sharks stitch him up, when they came round my house to get a statement from me. To be honest, we all drove like idiots, before the powers-that-be started taking all the fun out of it: black boxes, GPS tracking systems and a bunch of snake tongued policy lackeys, waiting to stab you in the back. The night before the crash, I'd been driving the car, recklessly, with Ozzy in the passenger seat, skidding round corners in the frost and doing handbrake turns, so it could have gone either way.

The funniest incident I remember, relating to police driving, was while on a night shift patrol with a girl called Tracy. She was quite funny: green, same as me, and she had a younger brother who had joined the army; we were always arresting him whenever he was on leave. She was another keen one and we had found a car-full of teenagers, parked up at Singleton Lake, smoking dope. Tracy nicked the driver and he asked if we could get his 'hot hatch' back to the police station, so it didn't get stolen, left out there all night. We were both new to the job and didn't know half the rules we were supposed to stick by, or quite a lot of the law. So the prisoner went with Tracy in the panda car (first rule broken – no escorting officer), back to the nick. I got into the bucket seat of his suped-up boy racer car ( second rule broken – not insured and not allowed to drive prisoners' cars as a favour) with his three mates, along for the ride.

When we had to stop at a set of lights, the young wide-boys started egging me on to test the car out and see how it compared to a 'gabber's ride'. I blipped the throttle a few times and looked across to my right, where Tracy's car sat level with us at the start point. The little steering wheel I held made the car very responsive, we were facing uphill on a wet road that curved to the right before the next set of lights sixty yards ahead: it was a drag race. The light flashed green and I floored it. The tires spun and I whipped the thing round the bend, easily taking the lead. I don't think the yobs in the back had really expected me to do it and I didn't know I was going to either, but it was very funny. Tracy was laughing, her prisoner didn't look that happy though; he just glared out of his window at us and we laughed again.

Well, I got his car safely back to the police station and drove it into the compound, only to be told to get it the hell out again. No, that was definitely not a part of the Kent Police service provision.

The best cop story I have, however, is from soon after I joined the Crime Investigation Team. It was a plain clothes role, so suit and tie or at least shirt and tie. I used to wear tweed jackets and my old school brogues; they still fitted me and were the best shoes I ever had. I was out in an unmarked car with a team-mate they called 'the Count', he looked a bit like Dracula's doorman. He loved driving and thought he was good at it (just like Simon) until he wrote a '4/0' pursuit car off by throwing it out of a junction, across the main road and into a hedge the other side.

The Count was driving us back to the station, after some boring inquiry, late one night and we came up behind this car with two blokes in. The way it was being driven suggested that they were up to something, and they didn't like having anyone behind them. It turned out that they were CAT Bs (category B target criminals) but we didn't know it and couldn't tell we had a situation at that point. Every turn off they made, we were there keeping up, while we put the call in to any uniformed patrols out and about. The scroats in the car caught on and tried to lose us; they drove down into Eureka Park Leisure Centre and we were right behind them as they hit the speed bumps; they had to make a decision at the mini roundabout before committing to one of the three car-park areas serving KFC, the fitness centre or the 'M20' night-club. My seatbelt was off and my hand was on the door catch, even before the target car made its move. They went for a U-turn, but we cut them off, and I was out of the Peugeot and running. I could see the driver's face now, a ruthless twist of hatred, he would have done

211

anything to get away that moment, as he slammed it into reverse and shot back, over the curb and part way through the wooden barrier, onto the freshly landscaped siding. His wheels were spinning in the dirt, but the car stayed put as I ran across in front of it to get to the passenger window. It was a warm evening and the window was wide open, the only thing I had on me was a mini can of CS spray in my jacket pocket, so I let them have it. The guide lines for police use of CS spray, as I remember, were: two short bursts, at a distance of three to five metres, to be aimed at the chest area only, so that the crystal particles should bounce off the chest into the face indirectly. My can was two foot away from the first scroat's face, two seconds worth straight into his eyes and the same amount in the drivers face – then again for good measure. It was all happening; the marked response car had made it and was skidding to a stop, right into the driver's door: that was good, as the driver couldn't get out – the passenger couldn't either, as the wooden barrier was wedged against his door. I was yelling 'Get out of the car!' and dragged the bloke head first through his window, forcing his face into the dirt, just as the Count appeared. I got a waft of CS and stepped up, as my bloke was being handcuffed by an enthusiastic officer, who'd not yet smelt it; the same thing was happening on the other side of the car and I stood a few paces out in the breeze and reviewed the beautiful carnage.

Everyone was coughing and spitting from the chemicals in the air, and it occurred to me that I had not actually warned anyone that I'd used the stuff. It was the most satisfying few moments of my Kent Police career, two bad guys banged up, several cops crying and no paperwork for me.

# CHAPTER 17: DECADE OF THE LAND ROVER

2002 began my first decade of the Land Rover. It started with a little SWB (short wheel base) Series IIA, fitted with an automatic V8 petrol engine. It only cost me £450 and it sounded too good, but the power delivery, to the rear wheels only, just wasn't useable. Starting was very particular, and it would stall if I tried to move off before it had had about a seven minute warm up period. I only kept it a few months before part exchanging, at a local garage, for a 1997 Land Rover Freelander, in royal blue. I really liked that car, but there was the issue: it *was* really just a big car. It was comfortable, okay, but had none of the rugged capabilities a Land Rover should have, like a towing chassis, tyres that grip on loose ground and some decent load space in the back – the Mini van had more capacity! The White Charger had had a better turning circle and could probably fit into a tighter gateway. It was a lovely car, but it had to go. I had driven a battered old Suzuki JLX around the Taurus Mountains in southern Turkey and quite liked it, so I decided to trade down to a little Suzuki Jimny; a genuine 4x4 with low ratio gear-box and dif. Lock, that could get in and out of anywhere and, with the back seats down and the front seats slid forward, you could get a small quad bike or a standard dining table in there. It never failed to start, and in the twelve years I kept it, we got through one new battery, two new exhaust systems and a couple of sets of tyres.

I drove Vottey and our newborn baby daughter, Rebecca,

home from the hospital in the Jimny. We used it for everything: I tied wooden posts to the roof bars, so that I could transport canoes down to the beach, and I only crashed it once, in the 75000 miles I got out of it. Once I left the police for good and gave up commuting, it became a less important toy. I passed it over to my mum, she got a year's more use out of it before boiling the head gasket, but we still got £400 for it, from a bloke who worked at Bob Fisher's garage (that was 'Norringtons') at the end of the Mad Mile.

In 2012, I'd felt it was time to splash out a bit, and I went and bought myself a 2003 model Land Rover Defender 130, double cab, high capacity pick up. It cost me £16.000 and had only 25000 miles on the clock, still on its original tyres too, I think. I put a few miles on, not only using it for logging up in the woods and towing livestock and machinery around, but also as a mobile camp site. I boxed out the containment bay to render it more suitable as a little living space under its canvas awning. Then I drove it across England, Wales, Ireland and Scotland, right to the Outer Hebrides and back. Everyone I met, wherever I went, said they loved that truck. It was awkward being so long; there was virtually no rear view through the clear vinyl patches (that really only let light through), so there was the same old concern: reverse parking by blind faith. I broke a tail light in the farm yard and I reversed into someone's car at a supermarket; it was a great truck, but I wasn't going to be getting around in it when I was eighty.

Land Rovers have got me in and out of trouble since I started driving them: none more so than Dad's old 110, a 1989 pre-Defender model. Since we first got hold of that reassuring looking block of steel and aluminium, we've pushed the boundaries, both on and off the road. Our farm land, on the edge of the North Downs, is clay. So it's bone dry in summer and a sticky mess come winter. It doesn't matter how good your tread is, once it's filled with clay from the first wheel spin, you don't have any at all. As soon as we got it, we took it down the steep slope from the top woods. Mum and I had to push, all the way back up, to help it as it crept along, with Dad at the wheel, spinning grass clay and leaf mould all up the sides; we weren't spared the showering either. It took us at least half an hour: forward a few yards, and then back a foot onto brushwood we'd laid behind each wheel. Forward again… and so forth.

Dad had this plan to cut trails all through the thickly wooded slopes, so we would be able to tour around the thirty-odd acre site, half of which being woodland and the other hillside grazing, with very few gentle parts to it. We did this, and used machinery to dig some of the tracks in, so that even the steepest natural bowls in the hillside could be accessed, in the dry at least. I made the mistake of driving down into the main coombe one wintery morning; there was a hard frost and I loaded up some logs. But I left it too long, so that the surface started thawing under the tree branches, before I tried to get myself out. That poor old Land Rover was trapped down there for over three weeks, while I tried several methods, including cutting trees out, and building up an escape route, using soil and rubble I dumper trucked over there. I cut two sections of the fence lines and gated them up, half way up the slope diagonally through the wood to the open pasture. If I could get it through the trees, we would be out on the hillside where I could get some grip in the couch grass. I could have got some speed up then to loop my way back onto the upper track.

Eventually, enough time without rain had gone by, that I was able to get her up the original track, almost to the top, well, three quarters of the way up, within winching distance of the upper level track. I had virtually finished my escape trail, but never had to use it in the end.

On a windy day in January 2013, I was parked up at the top of the hill, on my own, with the aim of chain-sawing a big old ash tree that had grown out over the fence line. We were having some high winds and I knew that one day this tree would come down and flatten our fence; then I would have to make a repair. I decided to take off the overhanging part, basically the upper two thirds, which included a section of the trunk and the whole canopy: everything from about fifteen foot off the ground. I've done a lot of chain-sawing in my time and ignored a lot of safety rules, but had never managed to hurt myself. I'd brought a big sturdy aluminium step-ladder with me, and put it out in the open field, under the part of the trunk where it started to curve out. I stood on the top platform, reaching out three or four feet beyond myself and started to make the cut.

I just started at the top, no undercut, no thought. The saw was halfway through when, without any warning, there was an almighty crack! Then I just felt my feet being dragged down through the ladder, with the noise of branches snapping and falling faster than gravity. The whole canopy crackled and crunched its way to the ground, leaving me hanging onto the remaining part of the tree. What remained of the trunk resembled a blue whale's rib bone and I was looking down from the high end, where I had both arms wrapped around it. The chain-saw was gone and there was no noise; the step-ladder was smashed and driven into the ground, like some twisted metal sculpture, and I knew I had nearly died.

The fact that I couldn't feel my feet was a bad sign. Looking down, the right leg of my boiler suit was ragged and my rigger's boot had a gash in it at the top of the foot. There was some kind of pink paste at the edge of the gash, which looked like wet shredded leather – but it wasn't. I worked my way down the trunk, arm over arm, until I could test a foot on the ground. A shot of pain hit me and jolted me out of that initial numb sense you get during a state of trauma: a coping mechanism, the senses are over-ridden so that pain registers as pressure, rather than screaming agony, so you can get yourself to safety. I tried the other foot and I couldn't use that either. So, I got my body down onto the mud and looked around. I was out there on my own, no-one knew I was up there, and it was so windy my voice wasn't going to carry. If I was badly injured (and I knew I was), then I needed to get off that hill quick.

I could see what had happened: because of the angle of the trunk at the point where I was cutting it, the weight, which I later calculated to be about seven tons (the weight of the old JCB or a small bulldozer), had caused the trunk to split with the grain, all the way to the base of the tree. It had done it so fast that the slice of trunk and the whole rest of the tree had come down as one mass. It was the curved slice of trunk that had smashed the step ladder, forcing a part of it through the top of my right boot, as the timber itself crashed across both my ankles. It had also taken the fence down with it, incidentally.

Always the practical man, I took the chain-saw in one hand and the double edged bill-hook in the other. On my knees, I dragged myself over the split trunk and across the thirty yards or so of field, towards the old Land Rover. I had to slither through a hole in the fence and then pull myself up into the driver's seat. I turned the key and it started: that was good.

There was nothing for it but to set her in second gear

and roll on down the hill into Stowting, then see how far I could get. It was about three miles home and there was only one junction where I might actually have to give way. My heavy boots helped and I could half clutch when I needed to. My broken right foot just rested on the accelerator pad, keeping it on an easy tick-over. When I wanted to throttle down, I had to grab my boiler suit at the knee and lift that leg up by hand. I couldn't use the brake at all.

Amazingly, I got home, and even made it up the drive to the farm gate. My mum arrived by car just then, and she went to open the gate for me. I said 'No, can you just take me to hospital please'. That was a fun ride; we couldn't go too fast, as with every bump we covered I was feeling it. I was still in the wheel chair we had commandeered, when the triage nurse eased my boot off. I didn't want to look at an open fracture, so I just asked her how it was. She said, 'There's no bone sticking out, but it is down to the bone.' I looked down, and that was enough for me. A three inch groove of missing flesh, with white lines in the bottom was what I saw and the morphine couldn't hit me quick enough.

Six hours of treatment later, nitrous oxide and very painful injections into all five tendons, plus half a dozen x-rays, and I was discharged with a plaster cast and a set of crutches that I wouldn't be able to use for weeks. I spent the rest of the winter laid out on the front room sofa, and dear little Rebecca camped out on the floor beside me every night. It was months before I could start to walk again: three vertical fractures of the right tibia and extensive ligament damage to both ankles; it could have been a lot worse.

Well would you believe it? Eighteen months later, I was back in casualty, having stitches to a deep gash in my forehead. This had happened up on the same hill, at the same woods, only this time it was a hornbeam tree.

During the winter before, several large trees had blown down, blocking the main track through the top of the woods. I'd just left them as they were, until summer time; then I decided to go up and start clearing, filling the old 110 as I went through. The main problem was a large ash tree that had come down flat. It had brought the upper parts of some lesser trees with it, leaving them planted so that the stands were bent over, all together like a twisted arch. There I was, hacking through the trapped branches with the double edged bill. One piece of, what I'd assumed was hazel (which is quite pliable and takes on a shape easily), and was about the width of a French stick, released. It smacked me square in the face, with the force of a medieval crossbow designed to take out an elephant. I gripped my brow in both hands as I went to my knees, holding firm, till I was ready to take stock of what had happened. My whole face tingled and hummed with pain and when I released the pressure from my hands, it was like a tap had been left dribbling and I knew it was bad.

I chucked the tools in the back quickly, then, for some reason, a couple of the logs I'd been cutting, splashing blood down my boiler suit as I went. I got in and started driving, hoping I could get down off the hill before I passed out. I made it back once again, without daring to look in the mirror till I was parked up. I couldn't really make out how bad it was, as the blood was thick and oozing, dripping off my nose like that red syrup they squirt over ice creams. I tried to clean myself up, but the skin was split an inch wide over my left brow and it was all swelling up, like a peach that had been dropped.

I thought I'd done well not to have been knocked out but I obviously needed stitches, so I called for an ambulance, then slumped into a chair to wait. The paramedics got there first; they called for support and two additional crews turned up. They seemed disappointed that they hadn't been called out to the scene itself and clearly would love to have been involved in a search and rescue mission off piste. They cancelled the Air Ambulance that had been scrambled, when I showed them that my neck worked fine, but still strapped me to a board and stretchered me off to the William Harvey. Four stitches later and a stack of codeine phosphate; then I was back on that front room couch, taking it easy for a couple of weeks, drinking tea and thanking my lucky stars it was summer this time.

It was quite a while before I could fit a crash helmet over my head, and I still have a bit of a lump there, but on the whole, I think I've come through both tree attacks quite well considering.

It's that left foot and ankle, from the original car crash, that's going to cripple me in time. Every fortune teller I've ever seen has told me I've got plenty of time on my card, so I'll just have to see how far I can go. All the while I can move, that's what I'm going to do, any way I can.

# CONCLUSION

That's not the end of the story, I'm sure. Land Rover announced that 2015 would be the final year of production for the world famous Defender model. There was never going to be the chance of owning a brand new Land Rover again and it was the only vehicle I'd ever really wanted to own, straight out of the factory. I was dismissing myself from Kent Police that same year, so reckoned I was due some kind of severance; a thank you to myself for suffering for fourteen years of my life: unwillingly; largely doing the unnecessary, for the often ungrateful.

I still used that old 110, with no tax, insurance or MOT, for over a year, before I was prepared to get my gleaming new Defender 90 station wagon out into the dirt. I just wanted to preserve it the way it was, for as long as it had that new car smell. It's 'Keswick green', with the traditional cream white top and standard steel wheels. It has fold-away seats in the back, the commanding view over that new style bonnet which houses the Ford Puma 2.5l diesel: and I'm keeping it for life.

I've had a clean licence for years now; miraculously I still have the original pink paper one, which I'm keen to keep a hold of. Anyway, I don't drive fast cars, I don't even drive fast. It's the others out there: the white van drivers, the school mums, those idiotic teenagers and twenty somethings, in their new Mini Coopers and whatever came after the Subaru Impreza.

I bought a 1971 Morris Traveller back in 1999; I thought it would be a replacement for the Mini van. Both cars are still sitting in my barn, waiting for the right time. What really appeals to me, as time is moving on, is an old American muscle car from the 1970s. V8 engine throbbing and grumbling, paintwork so deep you could dive into it, and those beautiful lines, like a bad woman in a heat haze.

The first job I took after my departure from the Queen's service was as a safari driver at Port Lympne Wild Animal Park. I was driving those old Bedford army trucks around the African Experience at about four miles an hour: towing a trailer and fifty passengers, while giving out a commentary that varied in enthusiasm and content, depending on how many times I'd been around that day. I only did one summer season. That same summer we had the Brexit vote; I had a bonfire party planned for the Saturday night, just after the country chose (by the narrowest of margins) to go it alone, and it was a fine evening. The two events were purely coincidental, but I managed to turn my do into quite a relevant social experiment.

I'm no partisan; I have my own conflicting views on popular politics and a British society. As Bob Dylan sang: 'I'll let you be in my dream if I can be in yours'. So I invited a cross section of opinionated friends and associates (who mostly didn't know each other). It was brilliant; I don't know what each and everyone was expecting, but they didn't get a copy of the guest list beforehand. There were hardcore outlaw bikers, right wing farmers, left wing university graduates, martial artists, disgraced and dispossessed ex-police officers, pagan Dark Age battle re-enactors and a couple of Romanian migrant workers. The funny thing was (despite a rain shower, my choice of old tape cassette music and the barbecued squirrel I served up), pretty much everyone seemed to be enjoying themselves. Most of them never came back, it's true, but at least they all got to experience a genuine bit of diversity, while we talked, drank and laughed about a brave new world.

# EPILOGUE

This work is based largely on material gathered from original diaries, journals and other records, compiled by myself, the author. Research for this book began in 2013, at the Police Federation Rehabilitation Centre of Flint House, in Goring, Berkshire. The work was composed and written in South East Asia: Phnom Penh, Chiang Mai, Chiang Rai and Mae Sai It was completed February 2018.

This, my second book, was inspired by the memories of certain great individuals:

Phillip Andrews, Warren Leggat, Anthony Keeble, David Bishop, Craig Tibbles, Martin Pointer, Christopher Carey and Duncan Taylor are sadly no longer with us on this journey. They are not forgotten.

> *The road is long*
> *With many a winding turn*
> *That leads us to who knows where*
> *Who knows when*
> *But I'm strong*
> *Strong enough to carry him*
> *He ain't heavy, he's my brother*

Ballard written by Bobby Scott and Bob Russell, made into a hit by The Hollies in 1969, re released in 1988

## THE END